MW01089504

ONE WOMAN'S WORLD:

The Columns of
Lenora Mattingly Weber

By Lenora Mattingly Weber

Edited by Betsy Edgerton

Betsy Edgerton [signature]

Image Cascade Publishing

One Woman's World:

The Columns of Lenora Mattingly Weber

By Lenora Mattingly Weber

Edited by Betsy Edgerton

Published by:
Image Cascade Publishing
420 Lexington Avenue, Suite 1402
New York, NY 10170
ImageCascade.com
Email: Support@ImageCascade.com

Cover Design: Madeline Nathaus

Typesetting: Madeline Nathaus

A CIP record for this book is available from the Library of Congress Cataloging-in-Publication Data

ISBN 978-1-955641-00-5

Printed in the USA

Dedicated to Rob Elder,

for his love and support

Contents

Contents

Introduction

By Betsy Edgerton

Lenora Mattingly Weber (1895-1971) was first a struggling short story writer and novelist, then a moderately successful short story writer and then, finally, a wildly successful girls series novelist. A mother of six—for decades, a single parent of six—she lived close to the edge financially until her children were grown.

Mrs. Weber was also a magazine columnist. She wrote "Mid Pleasures and Problems" for *Extension: The National Catholic Monthly* from 1946 to 1967, the century's tumultuous middle age. In that span of

Weber's long-running graphic for her column in Extension.

time she also wrote 23 novels (most for her teen girls series) as well as scads of short stories.

Her most beloved character, Beany Malone, was a contemporary of Nancy Drew in the boom years of fiction targeted to teen girls. In 1999, Weber fans brought those books back into print, spurring a mini-Weber renaissance as her work has been rediscovered—and savored. Her girls series novels and other books are back in print and her fans are active and engaged (even taking field trips to her Denver home). However, her shorter pieces—including the 266 columns she wrote for *Extension* magazine—have remained all but lost. Until now.

In a years-long project, I curated 50 of Mrs. Weber's best columns with the intention of bringing her wit, advice and worldview to a modern audience. These columns provide great insight into this writer's extraordinary life and times. But Mrs. Weber's columns were more than personal musings. She commented on the social issues of a large swath of the 20th Century, taking on such topics as religion and a woman's role in society. In the 1940s, she described post-World War II life in Denver, her home; in the 1950s she ruminated on the pros and cons of working mothers, and in the 1960s, she addressed Catholicism after Vatican II as well as racism and segregation.

And yet, the same writing style and messages that earned her lifelong fans for her teen novel series are legion in her *Extension* columns: charming anecdotes about a large, close-knit family; memorable characters brought to life through dialogue; pithy wisdom, delivered with a wink.

A personal note: By junior high school, I had made the transition from Laura Ingalls Wilder's *Little House on the Prairie* book series to Mrs. Weber's Beany Malone series, which was targeted to older girls. I unearthed the Weber books purely by accident, trolling the Young Adult stacks in the dim basement of my hometown public library, using my pre-pre-pre-Internet search algorithm: "Huh, that's an interesting book jacket; I wonder what the first paragraph says?" Little did I know that the books were in multiple printings, having turned a hard-working single mother into a popular novelist. Heck, I didn't know anyone else who'd ever read them.

I dabbled in the famous girls series books—Cherry Ames, Nancy Drew—but each book's plot was self contained, with little story arc throughout the series. The books lacked warmth and characters you could grow up with. The Malone family was different. Like the *Little House on the Prairie* series, you met the main character when she was young and followed her into marriage. But because the *Little House* books are so culturally omnipresent, they seem less personal to me. Mrs. Weber's books are more charming: The Malone house bustles with quirky family members, catching up over Sunday waffles or Monday meatloaf.

Covers in Norman Rockwell's style from Extension *magazine.*

The characters have a sense of humor; they grow and change over the course of the books.

Mrs. Weber's own story reads like something out of her novels. After her husband died in 1945, this mother of six supplemented her earnings as a fiction writer by writing her monthly column for *Extension*, which is still in publication. For her, the writer's life looked like this, she says in one of her columns: "I nursed babies and scribbled out plots. I packed paper, pencils and unfinished manuscripts in with baby nightgowns and diapers when I went to the hospital to have a baby."

For 21 years, Mrs. Weber churned out "Mid Pleasures and Problems" to pay the bills while she pursued her pride and joy: her fiction. The column was Mrs. Weber's first reliable paycheck. It was a

Lenora and her husband Al on their 25th wedding anniversary.

funding stream that Nonie, as Mrs. Weber's friends and family called her, relied on to shore up her unstable income. As her son David described it in his book *Nonie: An Autobiography and Biography of Lenora Mattingly Weber* (written partially by Mrs. Weber), she was paid "what was then a generous $200 per column."

"That monthly check from *Extension* was the first 'regular' money Nonie had ever earned. It seemed to move her across the threshold from boom and bust living to a steady although not exactly affluent life... Now, when an unexpected check arrived for [her fiction works'] royalties and foreign rights, it was not gobbled up by overdue grocery bills or back insurance payments," David Weber wrote. Tom Weber, the youngest son and last surviving child, echoed his older brother, telling me in 2021 that the money "saved our lives."

"Mid Pleasures and Problems" gave her a soapbox for her opinions as well as a writing space to try out themes for her fiction. The outlines of characters from Mrs. Weber's novels and short stories pop up in her columns. According to her son David, the only place her opinions "came to the surface in print" was in the column. She had a lot of freedom—as well as a deadline that hung over her head:

"[*Extension*] Editor Eileen O'Hayer gave Mother carte blanche with the column. She could cover any subject from national politics to neighborhood squabbles and family feuds. She could pontificate—not often—and she could fulminate—even less often," David Weber wrote. "But it was a monthly task that always seemed to catch her by surprise. As the deadline approached she would begin muttering that she just must get down to it. And no matter how late she left it, or how many midnight musings she gave to it as we sat sipping whisky and playing cribbage, 'Mid Pleasures and Problems' always seemed to get written and folded firmly into a half-size manila envelope and, usually, driven down to the main Denver post office so that it could get to Chicago on time."

A bit about *Extension* magazine: In the current niche-driven magazine publishing world, there's nothing with the cultural heft of the mid-20th Century *Saturday Evening Post*, the magazine that *Extension* most closely resembles, to speak to a broad range of Americans. Today *Extension* reads more like an alumni magazine than the general interest magazine it was in Mrs. Weber's column-writing days.

When Mrs. Weber was writing for *Extension*, it reached out to Catholics nationwide with news and features, as well as a call for donations for mission projects. The magazine was organized into sections for features, news, fiction, columnists, teens and children. *Extension*'s reach was both high-brow and low—it published weighty articles on thorny ecumenical issues and profiled politically active priests, but it also presented cooking and shopping features, complete with recipes and buying guides for clothes and tchotkes.

In an introduction to Mrs. Weber's first column in March 1946, the editors of *Extension* positioned her as one part Catholic, one part professional storyteller and three parts Mom:

"This brilliant writer has achieved something unique; she has successfully combined two careers—writing and motherhood. The mother of six children, she is thoroughly familiar with the task we have assigned her of writing about Catholic family life. Her skill as a writer plus her wealth of personal experience and her knowledge of Catholic philosophy guarantee articles that will be interesting and inspiring. Her own life has been a wondrous combination of laughter and tears, ups and downs, great crosses and greater courages."

Mrs. Weber lived her life like a reporter. She cast a wide net, listening, commiserating, sharing information. At the grocery store, on the bus, at her kitchen table—she was constantly gathering stories. Like a good journalist, she connected the dots, drew conclusions and painted her stories with colorful anecdotes. She was opinionated but open-minded, inspirational but pragmatic.

It bears mentioning that although Mrs. Weber's worldview grew more progressive over the 21 years she wrote her column, her language choice reflected her life and times along the way. She occasionally used terms that are now deemed offensive, regarding race, nationality and disability. I've trusted her intent while also modifying some of her wording. In a 1965 column about segregation, she used the n-word to quote a racist person, which I've altered, and I've changed the word Jap to Japanese.

She resolutely avoided the pulpit-ready writing style that characterized many of her columns when she wrote her girls series novels, declaring: "I know kids well enough to realize they'll shy away from a book that moralizes or preaches at them. The last thing they want is sermonizing drivel."

Mrs. Weber's best columns delivered a swift kick in

Her second column with Extension *in 1946.*

the pants. With her approach to modern foibles and challenges, she fell somewhere between a commentator and an advice columnist. The brisk— and sometimes brusque—tone of her writing makes her columns snappy.

Here she is in 1949 in a column about juvenile delinquents, adding some complexity to her standard hard-line advice-giving about child rearing:

"It is hard for parents and the critical world to realize that a child is not merely the sum of his parents or the product of his environment and training. He has an identity of his own, even as every dahlia, every colt, every diamond has. And just as some children are born color blind or tone deaf so do we have pathological personalities (not many, thank God!) who are utterly incapable of telling right from wrong. 'There are no delinquent children; there are only delinquent parents.' This [popular slogan] is but a half-truth. So before you condemn the parents for the misdemeanors of their child, think. Especially if you are a parent." ("Give Us Parents a Break," October 1949)

Mrs. Weber had empathy for the parents of troublemaking boys; her sons had their fair share of scrapes with the law. When her son Larry was 15, Mrs. Weber received the unpleasant news one night that the boy would be held overnight in the Detention Home, having been picked up by the police for "prowling a car" in the city park, according to her biography. Larry got a stern talking-to from police and no more, but Mrs. Weber took it hard. It wasn't the last time she'd get a late night call.

Early on, she let her readers know where she placed herself on the spectrum of career woman/working mother/homemaker. In a 1946 column of anecdotes about her struggle to steal some writing time in her chaotic household, she began to develop a persona for her readers that she would hone over the next two decades. Her message: "I love being a writer almost as much as I love being a homemaker."

Mrs. Weber was in good company with other mid-century fiction writers who wrote about their lives in magazine columns, as part of a genre called domestic chaos, or housewife writing, and this book rightly places her in that realm.

The most elite of those so-called housewife writers included Jean Kerr (the Broadway playwright), Shirley Jackson (famous for her short story "The Lottery") and Phyllis McGinley (a Pulitzer Prize-winning poet). Their columns were published in *Ladies' Home Journal*, The *Saturday Evening Post*

LENORE CATHERINE MATTINGLY
"OLD TOP"
*"She is debonair and pretty,
She is full of pep and witty."*
Longfellow Ent., '12; Basketball, '12, '13, '14, Capt. '15; Morey, '13, '14, Treas. '15; Annual Staff, '15; Vice-Pres. Spanish, '15; Vice-Pres. Senior Class, '15; Secretary Junior Class, '14; Chorus, '13, '14, '15; Vaudeville, '15; Morey Reading, '14, '15; Class Day Prog., '15.

Weber's high school yearbook photo.

and *Good Housekeeping*. These women lived and wrote at a different level. However they and Mrs. Weber all had something in common: They were juggling writing with motherhood, and they needed the money.

Mrs. Weber was the conformist of the group (who tended to focus on the hilarity of their lives). Mrs. Weber wrote seriously about topics they didn't—religion, race, sexuality—and her point of view was predictable for a Catholic magazine. In 1966's "Aphrodite Is Here Again," Mrs. Weber raged about a public that venerated a Madison Avenue manufactured version of female beauty, while tearing down the Virgin Mary.

"This is the frightening paradox, that all the

ballyhoo of advertising is on the girl making herself irresistible to the opposite sex and then, having made herself so, she is enjoined by anxious parents, deans of women, and the clergy to keep herself virginal. It is comparable to giving her a swimsuit on a tempting beach and then saying, 'You may frolic at the ends, but don't go in the water.'"

In the same column, she took a swipe at "The Pill," wondering briefly if it could be blamed also for this "pagan cult" of beauty and pleasure. It was an unhip point of view for the mid-1960s, but at the time, she was a 71-year-old Catholic grandmother. She'd been writing about teenage girls for decades, and used her granddaughter as a sounding board for her girls series plots, to make sure she didn't write like an old fogey. However, in the pages of *Extension,* she could be as much of a fogey as she wanted, though she rarely was, which makes her columns such a joy to read.

On some social issues—segregation, race relations, the modernization of the church—she was thoughtful and sometimes quite progressive. Some of Mrs. Weber's most effective columns were about writing. She loosened up in these columns; they have a lightness to them, as if she was glad for the respite from writing about Big Life Issues.

In 1967, after two decades of writing "Mid Pleasures and Problems," Mrs. Weber called it quits. Writing the column took away from her fiction. In her final column, Mrs. Weber shared the lessons she'd learned along the way.

"Even twenty-one years ago (when I was old enough to know better), I was unduly impressed by people with a sharp wit and a striking personality. Life taught me that the old-fashioned virtues which are not so showy—integrity, kindness, industry, gratitude and loyalty—wear better."

Mrs. Weber's columns wear well, too. Her message, although a product of her times, still buzzes with humor and vitality; her moral compass always pointed due north.

I hope you enjoy getting to know Lenora Mattingly Weber through her more personal writing. I've loved every minute of it.

—Betsy Edgerton
Chicagoland 2021

CHAPTER 1

Speaking of Families

March 1946

Beginning with this issue, Lenora Mattingly Weber, well-known novelist and short story writer, joins our regular staff. This brilliant writer has achieved something unique; she has successfully combined two careers—writing and motherhood. The mother of six children, she is thoroughly familiar with the task we have assigned her of writing about Catholic family life. Her skill as a writer plus her wealth of personal experience and her knowledge of Catholic philosophy guarantee articles that will be interesting and inspiring. Her own life has been a wondrous combination of laughter and tears, ups and down, great crosses and greater courage. We know you will enjoy this new feature.

How many times have you heard a middle-aged man say, "I wish now I'd taken out more insurance when I was young"? And he is apt to add, "Even though it would have been nip and tuck to make the payments, I wish I had. Because now I'd have security."

Going down on the streetcar the other day I sat by a woman friend of mine whose hair is almost white. She is a widow with her one son making his home in South America. She said, "I wish now I had had a real family when I was young." And she added, "Of course at the time we thought it was more important to buy a home and for my husband to get a start in business."

Now she has her lovely home; she has income enough to make her independent, but as I got off she touched my arm and said wistfully, "Won't you bring your daughter and her new baby over some day? I don't see many young people any more."

I thought of the middle-aged man realizing that his short-sightedness had left him without financial security for his old age. And here was this woman haunted with regret that her short-sightedness—or selfishness—had robbed her of happiness [and] security. Of the two, isn't this woman, and the countless thousands like her, more to be pitied than the short-sighted man and the thousands like him? Because Government and State have set up agencies to help the indigent of purse. But what agency can provide a telephone call for a lonely woman with a young male voice saying, "Say, Mom, how about meeting me downtown and helping me celebrate a raise?" Or perhaps a thirteen-year-old banging in the front door, saying, "Look here what I bought for you! A desk calendar so you always know what day it is."

For a family is solid insurance against being lonely and set in your ways and self-centered when you reach middle age and old age. Insurance against that panic a friend of mine confessed came over her when she wakened in the night with a sore throat and wondered whom she could call if she got really ill. Another alone-in-the-world woman told me that a cold chill went down her back whenever she passed a convalescent home and saw unattached, half-sick women sitting on the porch. Institutional care is usually as impersonal as a telephone operator's "Hello."

Having a family is fun. I sing no roundelay about the joy of childish prattle, or the patter of little feet. Because, more often than not, that joy is far over-balanced by working with a stubborn skin rash, or leaping up terror-stricken on a cold night at sound of a croupy cough—or worse yet, lying tense and wakeful listening for a rattly jalopy to come up the driveway while you picture mangled bodies or listen for a call from the police station.

Perhaps you've always said, "We want a family." Being young, you probably haven't read statistics about the human race dying out unless married couples have a certain quota. (Once it was four point four; I remember because that four-tenths of a child always puzzled me). But you want a family because you have an unanalyzed, deep-down-in-your-soul conviction that it's right with you and God.

And so you start having a family. And the budget is so lopsided what with haliver oil for the oldest and the ten-day hospital bill for the tiniest that you can't even think of a new winter coat. Every morning, whether you'd have a good night's sleep or not, there are the daily dozen to do (and I don't mean setting-up exercises). You skid over marbles as you hasten to the telephone. The wedding present vase you have cherished is broken by a tossed ball. You hurry up to church and light a candle with shaky fingers, praying that the culture the doctor took will prove it *isn't* diphtheria.

And perhaps about this time, friends who are not family-minded stop by in their new car on their way to the Thanksgiving football game. Being human, you feel a tinge of envy for their carefreeness; being young, you think how nice you'd look in that nubby tweed suit your friend is wearing.

All along the way you are made to realize that having a family these days is going against the popular current. Everything, from the fee the obstetrician charges to the small package of noodles you buy at the store, is geared to a small family. Houses are built with two—sometimes only one bedroom. No dining nook allows for more than two children—well, three if one is in a highchair. Heaven help parents of even one child when

3

they try to rent an apartment or house.

And folks will look at you pityingly. They will refer to a friend of yours as "Poor Ruth" because she is tied down with children and is tired-looking and shabby. You know they are "poor-ing" you behind your back. You will hear this, too, "I think a family is nice provided you can give children the advantages parents owe them." An insidious doubt creeps into your heart as to whether you are doing the right thing in going ahead and having a family.

Yes, you'll find it nip and tuck making the payments.

And then comes middle age. The "Poor Ruth" my friends used to refer to often stops by these days. Poor? I don't know a richer woman. Her days are brimming over with her own interests, family interests. She has kept not her figure, but her sense of humor. We laugh gaily about the time the cleaning woman we shared thought Ruth's husband's underwear was rags and used it in the mop. It was worn and patched but had to last, as Ruth said, till the latest baby was paid for.

And then during the war the childless woman started "poor-ing" us again. "Poor Ruth." "Poor Lenora." But they need not have. Even though we got up in the morning and went to bed at night with that feeling of mashed eggshells inside us. Even though we watched avidly for the mailman, and our knees were wobbly as we picked up the ringing telephone. Because as one unmarried career woman said to me, "I know you have worry and heartache. But at least your cup is full—and that's better than having it empty."

Yes, better.

CHAPTER 2

Mix Well Together

June 1946

It is late Monday afternoon now.

All day yesterday, through the Sunday hubbub of Mass-going, staggered breakfasts, and company to dinner, I thought longingly of today. Tomorrow, I vowed, I am *not* going to be the kind of a woman who lets her family interfere with her writing career to the detriment of both. Tomorrow I am going to be a writer and whip my new story into shape.

Because I knew that the love scene in the story would take both enthusiasm and energy, I went early to bed. But not early to sleep. For our house never really settles itself for the night until midnight or after. Then about two o'clock I heard the creak of the back porch door, then footsteps through the house.

Investigation proved it to be our niece who, as stewardess on an airline, had just got in from San Francisco. All our beds were full but we tugged the youngest out of his, shoved him in with his brother, searched his bed to be sure his pet white rat was not snuggled somewhere in it. Though my niece said concernedly, "Now you get right back to bed," and I did, I didn't get right back to sleep. We don't when we reach the gray-haired stage.

So this morning had a dragging take-off with everyone visiting over pancakes and coffee. Then ordering groceries, cajoling a plumber to fix a leak. And the youngest had tossed off as he left for school, "Hey, Mom. Sister wants us to wear white pants and a white shirt for the P.T.A. program tomorrow." Oh-oh! That meant salvaging his white shirt out of the already-packed laundry bag, washing it, letting down the hem in his First Communion pants.

I had just reached my study door—feeling not too adequate at tackling the love scene—when relatives telephoned from a town two hundred miles away to ask me to find them a hotel room for the night. That took over an hour of telephoning. I was still at it when my young married daughter said from the doorway, as she squirmed into a bright green coat, "I've got the bottle propped up on the pillow but will you sort of check it?" With living quarters the unsolved problem of the day, my daughter, her husband and their brand-new baby have taken our front bedroom and alcove upstairs. And baby carriages had been advertised in Sunday's paper. There on the couch in my study was the baby, gurgling her eleven-o'clock feeding. Was there ever a grandmother who could keep from leaning over a grandchild and crooning out nonsense just to bring a wide, dripping grin?

But at last things were quiet and I was just unveiling the typewriter when the door opened and the niece and my second son—tall, and with hair that waves unless it's cut short—came in. He said beaming, "I got some fresh shrimp. How about French-frying them for lunch?"

I started to say, "Let's just have sandwiches." But this boy was in a Japanese prison camp forty-two months on a scant rice diet. . .I reached for the eggs to make a batter—

Sometimes in exasperation I say between set teeth, "God help the woman who tries to write at home." Often I chuckle ruefully, thinking of how when the children were little and I was forever tying shoes, sterilizing bottles and wiping noses, I declared optimistically, "But when the children can do for themselves, I'll have time to write."

That remark was made in ignorance as well as optimism. For it is an immutable law of life that once you have carried a child under your heart, your heart is forever attuned to his—his griefs, his elations, his problems. Whereas small children demand of your physical strength, older ones take of that inner strength of mind and spirit.

I remember a time when my typewriter was stilled for days by my third son—also with hair that waves blackly—showing me the notice that he was to report for his Navy physical in two days.

I remember an evening when I had settled myself for a few hours concentration on a story, and my daughter, then twenty, came in. "Mother, I'll only bother you a minute. But what would you think of my getting married in October?"

But, always upon a close searching of my heart, I realize that all this griping I do about not finding time to write is merely surface griping. For, deep inside of me, I feel that I am singularly blessed by God. I even have a guilty feeling that I—even as all women who juggle a career and family—have more than my share of "enriched" happiness. For we women have all the heart-filling ups and downs of family life.

Life, after all, is pretty much like climbing a mountain. No doubt the one who travels alone, keeping his eyes only on his goal, gets to the top sooner than the one who takes time out to enjoy the going, to match his step with others.

If I had the choosing to do over, I would never choose to be only a writer. Success for even a career woman must be two-sided—her career side, her woman side. And instead of pursuing both to the detriment of both, she pursues them—perhaps more slowly, more falteringly—even fumblingly—to the enrichment of both.

So now it is late afternoon, and the thirteen-year-old calls excitedly, delightedly from the stair landing, "Mother, come here! Maggie's had her kittens—four of them—in the linen closet."

Oh well. I think, as we prepare to move Maggie and family (in spite of Office of Price Administration rulings) out of her chosen apartment to a closet corner, now *tomorrow* will be a nice, long day when I can get at that love scene with eagerness and ardor.

CHAPTER 3

They Say

October 1946

Last week my neighbor and I paused to rest after a tiring bout of digging plantain out of our front lawns. The lawns had been put in new last year and had come up fresh and weed-free. My neighbor kept puzzling, "I can't imagine where this awful crop of plantain came from." We knew it hadn't come from the fertilizer because it had been weed-proofed. "I'll bet," he concluded finally, "the seed blew in on those strong spring winds we had."

. . ."We can't let Mary Smith in our club. *They say* she makes trouble in every club she belongs to.". . . "*They say* the Negroes are bumping the whites off the streets in Los Angeles.". . ."*They say* that all this sending money and food to the starving in Europe is just a racket.". . ."*They say* the Jews have all the big jobs in Washington.". . ."You know the Riordans on the corner? *They say* those boys steal anything they can get their hands on.". . .

Just as the gusty spring winds pick up and toss weed seeds onto every lawn, so does this tossing about of they-says plant harmful, sturdy, vicious seeds.

For years, I must confess, I was a they-say person. I did my share of tossing on they-says, just for the lazy fun of saying something exciting or startling. I let they-says take root in my mind. And then, several years ago,

9

a small incident occurred that jerked me up short as to the individual harm, as well as the mass harm, they-says can do.

I had taken time off from my writing, to lunch with a friend we will call Pauline, who does historical writing. In a year's time we had developed a rich and stimulating friendship. Over our iced-tea she said, "We met each other thirteen years ago. I wonder why we weren't friends sooner."

I was ashamed to tell her the truth. When I first met Pauline, another person warned me emphatically, "Don't have anything to do with her. *They say* she has the meanest tongue of any woman in town." And so, although Pauline and I had much in common, I let myself be scared out of a friendship with her.

Sitting there at the luncheon table across from Pauline, whose tongue I had never found sharp, I felt a deep disgust with myself. Why had I let that nebulous, mythical, malicious they-say cheat me out of years of give-and-take friendship?

Perhaps you have heard the story of the little tyke in his high chair with a dish of spinach before him? And how to his mother's over-all statement of, "All little boys like spinach," he banged on his high chair and challenged, "Name me just two."

This unfair-to-me, unfair-to-Pauline incident started me thinking. Right then I decided that from there on out whenever a sweeping they-say statement came my way, I would challenge, "Give me just two proofs. Or even one." Right then I vowed that, in my small way, I would stop every ill-founded, vicious they-say from blowing on—and on—and on.

For they-say opinions are seldom opinions. They are merely prejudices which are planted in ignorance, and thrive in ignorance.

Do you suppose that the virulent criticism and condemnation of our Church comes from the ones who have first-hand knowledge, or are willing to make an effort to get it? No, they are prejudices borne on the they-say winds. . ."*They say* any divorced Catholic can remarry if he pays the bishop five-hundred dollars." (My butcher actually said that to me one day.) The way to uproot such a rumor is to answer, "Name me just one bishop who took the five-hundred and let the divorced Catholic marry."

Do you suppose the men who were talked into wearing the Klan sheet-and-pillow-case would put it on so willingly if their minds weren't weed-grown on they-says? "*They say* the Jews have a stranglehold on all business." "*They say* the pope wants to rule from the White House." "*They say* if the Negroes aren't lynched down South, it wouldn't be safe for white women on the streets."

How the wind does blow!

Since I have "alerted" myself, I am amazed—yes, and frightened!—at how casually on street corners, over luncheon tables, during Sunday drives these they-says are tossed off, at how casually they take root—and how un-casual is the ever-spreading destruction they do.

I have found out, regretfully, that while making vows is easy, carrying them out is uncomfortably hard. My one-woman campaign against the they-says has not been easy. For I am not a challenger by nature. A friend once very rightly commented that I was like a friendly pup who wanted people to pat him on the head.

So that when a week or so ago at a gay dinner party, someone remarked, "*They say* that on our Darktown bus the Negroes deliberately bump and push the white people around," I had to swallow twice before I answered, "That isn't true. I've ridden the Darktown bus a lot and I wasn't bumped or pushed around any more than on our Whitetown ones."

But there I had my own knowledge as an uprooting tool. You can't uproot prejudice with ignorance. The they-says that are confounding to a politically lazy mind like mine are the ones which take good old statistics to kill. For one person cannot be well-informed on every subject. Yet you can always meet prejudice by a reasoning opinion. You can always say, "I doubt that. Where did you get your information?"

And you can always hold tight to your own faith in the good of humanity. Not long ago I found myself greatly outnumbered in a heated argument which started on, "This fool idea of us here in the United States thinking we can feed and take care of the rest of the world." I was one of the misguided fools who believed it was our duty. To Catholics this is not a new idea. We have cut our teeth on supporting our missions. Yet we have always had to meet the skeptics who say, "But look at the poor we have right here. Charity begins at home."

We have been taught the answer to that. Charity begins at home, but it doesn't end there. The same answer is good now.

No, we cannot all be encyclopedias of information. Nor can we stop the gusty winds of they-say. But we can keep on patiently uprooting the seeds that blow helter-skelter; we can meet a they-say head on with a "Who says? How do they know?" We can be like the little fellow in the high chair and look the spreader of prejudice in the eye and challenge, "Name me just two."

CHAPTER 4

Double or Nothing

February 1947

"You don't know of an apartment we could rent?"
. . ."Do you know of a house we could get for three months?". . ."Have any of your neighbors got an extra room?". . .These greetings have become about as common from friends or acquaintances as the stock, "Hello, how are you?"

The For Rent column in the daily paper is now practically nonexistent. Families and relatives—even friends—have been doubling up for the past year or two. And, in spite of plans for housing projects, it looks as though this situation will continue another year or two.

Our morning paper carries one of these "Please help me solve my problem" columns. Again and again, along with our breakfast coffee, we read letters from members of these doubled-up households, who write of desperate grievances, of boiling-over resentments. Young husbands seething over a mother-in-law's discipline of children. Mothers wailing over selfish, slovenly daughters-in-law. The countless, daylong frictions resultant of doubled-up living.

My own daughter, her husband, and her two small babies have our upstairs front room and alcove. A baby's play-pen almost takes over our living room; the toilet chair scrapes our shins in the bathroom. We walk around a clothes-dryer in the upstairs hall. My daughter and her husband play cards with other couples who are living with either his folks or her folks; one couple is living in the dark basement of the husband's aunt's house. None of this doubling up is from choice—oh, certainly not from choice. But from necessity of these abnormal times.

It is abnormal—almost un-American for young married couples. Hasn't the wife, from the time she was six, played at keeping house? Part of the ecstasy of courtship is the interwoven plans of "A home of our own." And it is equally abnormal for the older generation. For we have turned the page and are ready for the quiet chapter of our life. We have lived through the chapter where babies yelled for bottles; where we dared not put a bouquet of flowers—or even our glasses—on the low cobbler's bench.

What is the answer? (As I write this, a young man in the office where I have a cubby-hole for writing, stopped and said, "What can you say about it, except that it's plain hell?" His face is tightly bitter. He and his wife and two children are living in four rooms with his wife's mother and stepfather.) My only answer is that old worn-thin adage: What can't be cured must be endured. What can't be cured must be made endurable. For right now it's *double or nothing* and no alternative.

How to make it endurable? From our own experience, from the tragic experiences I have listened to, it seems to me that two traits can shake this, as well as make almost any unendurable situation endurable; honesty and a sense of humor.

I realize, of course, that our family has, by circumstances, been a little better "conditioned" for such doubled-up living than some. We have always been a big and overlapping family. All through my married life, we have had more under our roof than the immediate family. Out-of-town friends, a niece or nephew attending school, a grandma that we hurried to take the first cup of coffee to in the morning. Both parents and children in big families

14

acquire a flexible give and take.

But to get back to how honesty and a sense of humor can make doubled-up living endurable.

To begin with, meet the issue honestly. Why pretend that doubled-up living is ideal? Say to the young couple, "I know this is a poor substitute for having your own home." Go even further and, admit that it has its drawbacks for you, too. (Sometimes I wonder if this frank, un-Pollyannish attitude wouldn't help in world affairs, now that the world's roof is shrinking, and we are rubbing such close elbows with other nations.)

Discuss frankly all arrangements. If the mover-in family is to pay a flat rate, settle it clearly just what they are paying for, be it for room and board, with their paying for their own laundry and toll telephone calls? If you have a "kitty" where each person puts in on a ratio basis, replenishing it when the kitty meows for more funds, have it well-established as to whether the cleaning woman, the new snow shovel, the replacing of light bulbs comes out of that or not.

Air your grievances. Don't let them rankle and fester. It's far better to say with gentle honesty, "Now, look I see your side, but on the other hand—" Nothing clears the air like a laying of cards on the table.

A sense of fair play wears far better than the dubious satisfaction of martyrdom. Martyrs have their place, but hardly in a crowded household in the year of our Lord, 1947. So many of those "Please-help-me" letters in the morning paper are written by martyrs whose crown has come to pinch. . ."I started out doing my daughter-in-law's washing and now she expects me to.". . ."I let my wife's brother use my car, and now he's bashed in a fender. . ."

Be fair about the division of work. In our house, because I love to cook, and because that time of evening the babies take the most care, I come hurrying home in time to get dinner. I am a fizzle at keeping things orderly, and it is a joy to step into a house that my daughter keeps "picked up."

The same sense of fair play will keep reminding you of the compensations, which may or may not balance the disadvantages of doubled-up living. There are compensations. In these parlous times, with coal shortages, car shortages and soaring expenses, it gives one a physical, even a psychic comfort at times. As in frontier days, when folks doubled up for safety against foes.

And, above all, keep your sense of humor. A good laugh at your own expense is hardier armor than dignity or sensitiveness. Rather raggedly and thinly, my husband and I laughed the first time one of our children said to us, when he had company, "Now if you two will just fade—" In doubled-up living you have to learn to "fade." That, by the way, is one of the hardest lessons oldsters have to learn.

I've learned, too, that family teasing lets off family steam. How the family rib me! About losing important letters, about liking pancakes for breakfast, about always vowing I'm going to bed early and not getting there until long after midnight. But steam that isn't let out can form an eruption.

And, as usual, when times are abnormal, this making of crowded living conditions livable rests more easily on the women than on the men. Partly because the men are out of the home more. Partly because men are, by and large, more obtuse, less sensitive to the nuances of relationships. But, because men are more chameleon-like when it comes to taking on the color of their womenfolks' happiness or unhappiness. It behooves women to work hard at this *double or nothing* way of living. It behooves them to hold tight to the hope of *there'll come a day* when life will be normal, And when rough edges of personalities are rubbed raw, it behooves the women to murmur fervently, "God give me wisdom and strength," and scratch around for something to laugh about.

CHAPTER 5

"Don't Miss Tomorrow's Thrill-Packed Episode"

April 1947

I read *David Copperfield* to my older children. Gathered together, after the dinner dishes were done, we read it. We chuckled over "Barkis is willin' "; we cried over Dora's death.

Several months ago, on a wintry night, I said to my two youngest boys, aged fourteen and nine, "Let's read *David Copperfield.* You'll like it." And so I read. They squirmed as I read, their interest lagging, and finally the younger one burst out, "Well, gee, when is something going to happen?"

It gave me pause, a sad, regretful pause. Were these children not to know the warmth of Father Flynn's books, the thrill of *Horatio at the Bridge,* the tugging sorrow over *Black Beauty,* because of what radio programs, the movies, the comic books have done to their taste buds? Had they dulled their mental taste, just as a continuous overuse of catsup does to its user?

The Triple Threat—radio serials, movies, comics. (Why are they called comics when they are not comic but only highly-condensed thrillers?)

17

But I place the heaviest blame on radio serials. For you can, without being thought too unnatural a parent, limit your children's movie-going to one night a week. Then, too, our Legion of Decency [a Catholic group that monitored movies for objectionable material] has lent a helping hand to parents in the movie problem.

The comics are bad. Cheap paper, garish colors, unartistic art work, sensational writing. And show me a child who doesn't "eat 'em up." But they cost a dime at the corner drugstore, and dimes don't grow on the bushes in the average family's front yard.

So I placed the heaviest guilt on the radio serials. The radio, like the poor in the Bible, is always with us. And children learn, along with their A.B.C.'s, the frequencies of the radio dial.

That wintry evening, holding the spurned *David Copperfield,* I looked at my two with sick and angry defeat. After a continuous dose of *Superman, Hop Harrigan, Tom Mix, Lone Ranger*—ad infinitum, of course. Dickens's rounded rhetoric, his leisurely building of suspense, his nuances of humor and pathos seemed so tedious that they demanded, "When is something going to happen?" Conditioned as they were to dialogue that goes, "Come clean, sister, or you'll take a cozy little walk to the hot seat," Dickens's slower dialogue seemed deadly.

I have talked to different mothers and fathers about the harm of the radio serial on young minds. "Well, it's no worse," one said, "than the soap-operas women listen to."

No worse—no better. Thousands of housewives iron to Stella Dallas sobbing her way through life after an erring past. They vacuum while a maudlin melody ushers in unfaithful husbands, scheming friends, psychopathic step-daughters. *Kyrie eleison!* A physical or emotional crisis as a come-on so that these thousands of housewives will tune in tomorrow.

But these women are beyond the plastic years. Their taste buds, dulled by this emotional catsup, are beyond saving—if, indeed they were ever existent.

But what about our eight-to-sixteen-year-olds? Can we or can we not take the catsup bottle away?

My quarrel is not with the morals of these Monday-through-Friday serials. Superman, Captain Midnight, "Tawm" Mix are always on the side of law and order, always fighting the good fight. And the Lone Ranger. "Never has there been such a champion of justice in the pages of history." (I'm not sure I'm quoting the exact words inasmuch as I always hear it over the hub-bub of meal-getting.)

And that reminds me of a story a social worker told me. She had a class of Spanish Americans who came from down close to the railroad tracks. At Easter time, she thought it most relevant to tell them the moving story of the Crucifixion. They were emotionally carried away by it, so much so that one little boy sobbed out, "Why couldn't the Lone Ranger come on Silver and shoot up the bad men?" Sacrilegious? Perhaps. But it certainly shows that our young are more familiar with the miracles of the Lone Ranger than the miracles performed by the Man of Galilee.

My quarrel is simply with the fact that these radio serials provide excitement in too large and unnatural doses. Too many screams of terror, too many guns banging, too many villains, too many forms of torturing death. It not only makes real fiction seem verbose and ponderous, but it makes the normal placidity of real life seem like stagnant backwater. It is too much emotional catsup which ruins their taste for the solid bread of life.

It does this, too. It creates a mental laziness for reading the printed page. The lost art of reading would be a great loss for the child of today—an even greater loss for [the] adult.

It is this same mental laziness, as well as

physical, that makes us a nation of spectators rather than participants. More and more, we demand that our entertainment be ladled out to us. It is easier to see the movie, *Song of Bernadette*, than to read the thick volume. Yet we get more *good*, more *satisfaction*, out of participating in our own poor brand of tennis, singing, horseback riding, than sitting comfortably watching or listening to professionals. . .Just as we Catholics are constantly enriched by church-going because we *participate* in the Mass. We don't merely sit comfortably while someone preaches, while a soloist performs.

But to get back to the "What to do" about these corrupting radio serials. We can control them and counteract them.

We can do our utmost to control them at the source. I believe our voices would be heeded if we wrote to radio sponsors and said, "Tone them down. We think they are overloaded with excitement."

Then we can do some controlling in the home. Just as we would reach out a detaining hand if we saw a young child covering everything on his plate with catsup. We can say firmly, "Now too much is too much. You can listen to one of these serials—but not to all of them. So take your choice."

I know a mother who forbade her child to listen to any of them. But that wasn't successful. For he resented being an unhappy exception. On the way to school, he'd demand of his friends, "How'd they get out of the quicksand last night?" (No doubt the quicksand had been up to their chins when the announcer bleated, "Don't miss tomorrow's thrill-packed episode.")

Often ridicule does wonders. I've noticed that since I've referred to Tom Mix as "Tawm," my youngest looks a little foolish every time Tom's faithful sheriff addresses him as "Tawm." Another member of the household took to mimicking the announcer who frenziedly introduced Superman with his "Ready to leap tall buildings at a single bound!" with a "Ready to leap tall corn at a single bound!" At the end of one program the fourteen-year-old admitted, "That sure is tall corn."

And we can stubbornly seek to immunize them against becoming too saturated with the roar of six-shooters, atom bombs that will destroy civilization unless Captain Midnight gets there in time. We can stubbornly take them down more leisurely lanes of reading—even if they do squirm uninterestedly at first. What young mind wouldn't succumb to *The Yearling, Treasure Island, My Friend Flicka?*

That's the only answer I see. I see no hopes of immediately stopping the tide. Our only hope is to save them from being engulfed by it by fortifying from within—as one of the hot breakfast cereals advertises on the radio.

CHAPTER 6

This Strange Inhibition

January 1948

Last week I started to write a note to a woman friend who has only a few months more to live. I started the usual light patter of, "Sorry to hear you're under the weather—" and then I paused. What were empty phrases to a woman who knew that she was about to enter the vast forever? Yet, I felt a certain squeamishness about opening my heart and talking of God's arms and the peace that passed understanding—of telling her that I would pray for her.

I remembered that we had talked often of politics and income tax and cold shots—but never once of God. We had talked, as most folks talk nowadays, of things that didn't matter, carefully skirting things that did matter. I sat wondering why. Why did my generation, which prides itself on being conversationally uninhibited, have this strange inhibition about talking about God?

We have always chuckled deridingly about what we called the hush-hush attitude of our mothers and grandmothers toward sex. So in conversations we toss about words like "divorce," "pregnancy," "frustrations," without realizing that we have the same hush-hush reticence, even embarrassment, about talking about our belief in God, our solace in prayer, our striving for virtue. Not that my generation doesn't toss the word God about, but the "Oh Gods!" and the "My Gods!" are used in the same tone, that we say, "Oh nuts!"

I asked myself why. I asked some of my friends why. One said she thought it was a hang-over of the revolt against Puritanism. Another said she thought it was because we had known so many hypocritical holier-than-thous who were always brandishing Bible verses about. Another said she thought it was because of the wave of cynicism that seemed to ride along with the would-be intelligentsia. In other words, it isn't "smart" to be religious.

One serious-thinking friend who is deeply devout inside in spite of a blithe and erudite manner, confessed with some shame, "There are two types of people who make me act as though I'm irreligious—when really I'm not. One is the overly sanctimonious type. This unctuous palaver irritates me so that I act flip and godless. But even worse than that, when I'm with a group who sneers at all religions and looks upon an abiding faith as something adolescent and illiterate, I'm not courageous enough to step up and say, 'I think it's wonderful. I shouldn't weather through without help from God.' So there you are—in my case it's contrariness or worse—cowardice."

In my own case, I was always fearful as a child of being thought goody-goody. I knew that kind and they weren't much fun. As a young woman, I knew the prissy, narrow-minded thou-shalt-nots. And I didn't think much of them either. (I still think it's a great pity that so many "good" people are soggy and humorless. They shouldn't be; their very faith should tend to make them leaven and sparkling.)

Even so, these attitudes of the friends I questioned or my own scarcely bear analyzing. Our revolt against Puritanism was against its joyless, prim austerity. Never against its belief in God. It is true there are religious hypocrites, just as there are religious crackpots, both harmless and vicious, who come to your door with the question, "Do you know that thousands now living will never die?" Both the hypocrites and the crackpots rightly fill us with an embarrassed realization that God and our love for Him should be on a more dignified plane.

But just because we don't want to be classed with either of these—or even with the holier-than-thous—is still no excuse for us to hide our Faith like a family skeleton.

In that delightful and heart-warming book, *The World, the Flesh, and Father Smith,* Father Smith remarks, "We are afraid to be ourselves in crowds because we are afraid not to be like what we think our neighbors are and our neighbors are afraid not to be like what they think we are. And so everybody pretends to be less pious, less virtuous, less honorable than he really is."

Yes, and some of us, fearful of being thought pious, pretend to be impious. I think it is time we shed this hypocrisy. I believe the world—even our own small sphere—is more hungry for God-solace than we realize. In a small gathering of friends, if one is racked by a cough, everyone, immediately solicitous, offers his or her favorite panacea for it. So why should we not, when another friend is racked with worry and grief, pass on to him the only healing we found on nights of heavy anxiety—that simple prayer, "Into Thy hands, O Lord—"?

At a luncheon table for four one day, a friend asked us all how we interpreted that line, "The meek shall inherit the earth." It started a discussion that was *real* and far more stimulating than the usual chit-chat about the high price of eggs, what some one's bright grandchild said or how laundries lost pillowcases. For once we didn't skitter away from the word "God." The ice broken, we talked of prayer, temptation, atonement for sins.

I think it's time we stopped being inhibited about the

realest things in life and death. It's time we stopped thinking it's smart to pretend to be irreligious when inwardly we are sustained by religion.

I don't mean that we should stand with clasped hands on Main street or that we should cram our own beliefs down unwilling throats. I do mean that it is disloyal to ourselves and cravenly disloyal to our Best Friend to pretend we don't know Him. I think we should remember that He said, "He that shall deny me before men, I will also deny him before My Father who is in heaven."

CHAPTER 7

"Come into the Kitchen"

August 1948

Thank heavens, the era of those soulless kitchens is passing. There was a time when architects and contractors gave us kitchens that were as efficient and unwasteful of space as an antiseptic telephone booth. It was considered a disgrace to have a dishcloth, an onion or a butcher knife showing. I remember a horrified friend saying to me once, "But don't you have a vent over your stove to eliminate cooking odors?"

As though the smell of lamb stew or gingerbread in a house was a heinous offense!

There was a time when it was considered a gentle disgrace for a family to eat in the kitchen. And, as for seating company at a kitchen table—well, it just wasn't done.

Thank heavens, it is done now. Families are being drawn back to the healing and cheering warmth of the kitchen. Women are realizing that, when space is at a premium, a dining room scarcely pays its way. The emphasis is on easy family living, rather than entertaining.

Some years ago when we moved into this home, we decided to combine the cigar-box dining room and living room for greater breathing space. It means that any dinner party over six or seven has to be served buffet style. There have been times, to be sure, when I have regretted not having a dining room. Entertaining is more scrambled, what with having to set up tables and hunt chairs from all parts of the house. But day-by-day living is simpler when the mother can slide food from the stove onto the table in the kitchen corner; when she can sit at the table and say, "Who's got a long enough arm to reach the coffee pot?"

In remodeling, we gave more loving thought to doing over the kitchen than to any other room. Walls and woodwork of lemon yellow, with red leather (imitation) on dining nook benches, and red linoleum on table and cupboard tops. Because I like something between my feet and linoleum, I have oval rag rugs on the floor which can go to the laundry.

A newspaper-artist friend painted a mural on the wall over the table. It's of an old prospector and his two packed burros, heading over the beckoning mountains. It's typical of the West, but so is it typical of all human hearts with hope eternal. We all took a few brush flicks at it. Our two youngest boys did some of the cacti in the foreground. Because I didn't think the skillet, strapped onto the lead burro, had a long enough handle, I made it longer. (I didn't want the poor old prospector to burn his hand.)

Some families are too large for anything but a wide-open dining room table. Ours used to be. But dining room or no, the kitchen is still the heart of the home. It is still the symbolical flame under a simmer pot to which tired, hungry, bruited homecomers are drawn. Here the twelve-year-old heats his soldering iron. The teen-age daughter tries out the new recipes she learns in Homemaking. The whole family gravitates around the lighted oven on chill and bleak mornings when the furnace is slow in starting. On the oven door you warm the baby's clothes to put on after his bath.

I wonder how many lonely soldiers have been sustained by their "kitchen memories." Soldiers who were asked into our homes always shed their stiff shyness with their coats when they come into our kitchens. It started them talking about "mom" and "back home."

I wonder how many courtships have burgeoned with the man saying to the girl, "you wash and I'll wipe." And surely the clink of glasses and suds in a dishpan is a more salutary background than the clink of glasses and suds on beer glasses in a smoke-filled tavern.

I wonder how many women have alleviated their griefs by reaching for a yellow bowl and mixing spoon. Many's the good "mad" I've worked off by mopping the kitchen floor. Even a child's cantankerous mood is visibly lessened by his stepping into the safety zone of the kitchen and spying a pan of cinnamon rolls. I remember my two oldest sons recovering from the mumps, asking wistfully the day they were allowed to get up, "Now can we go out into the kitchen with you?" And you've noticed, haven't you, how little children prefer playing with an egg beater in the kitchen to the expensive mechanical toys in a playroom?

Looking back over the years, I can remember far more intimate opening of hearts over a cup of coffee in my kitchen than in the living room. Family problems seem to smoothen when thrashed out over a kitchen table. And you can almost "kitchentest" your friends. If you feel reluctant to say, "Come on into the kitchen while I ice a cake," there's something lacking in the friendship.

A kitchen should be friendly. I don't mean that it should be old-fashioned and inefficient. The average housewife spends too many hours in it. I'm all for self-wringing mops and toasters that do our remembering for us. But I'm also for a pot of chives and parsley on the window sill, a string of red peppers within reach for chile; for a radio so that ironing can be done to music. I'm for kitchens having enough "allure" to compete with the dice games in the alley and the gatherings at the corner drugstore. Maybe a strong kitchen influence could help solve the growing and frightening problem of juvenile delinquency.

CHAPTER 8

Gratitude is the Music of the Heart

November 1948

Many years ago an older woman said to me that she had found that the infallible test of a person's character lay in his ability to say "Thank you" graciously and promptly.

At the time, I took issue with that. I thought it quite unfair to judge any person by what seemed to me mere polite externals.

But with the passing of the years I have come to see the wisdom in her remark. For I have realized that a heartfelt, "It was lovely of you—" or "You don't know how much I appreciate this—" is not merely an external gloss but something that comes from an attitude of mind. It is the words to the music of gratitude in the heart.

You have all experienced, I'm sure, that disheartening and flat feeling when you have had a guest in your house and it has meant a shifting of beds and extra dashes to the store, not to mention opening the jar of apricot preserves you were hoarding and then the guest leaves without any or, at best, a brief and perfunctory word of appreciation. And you have all spent weeks and then months after mailing a graduation present

31

to California or the christening gift to New York, of wondering if your gift had been lost in the mail? And, finally, in answer to your query, comes the faint and belated chord of gratitude. "He gives twice who gives in a thrice." It could be said, "He thanks twice who thanks in a thrice."

And who can blame anyone for staying his hand when he finds his time and money and effort have sounded no music of gratitude?

I had a neighbor and friend once and, even yet, when we meet we chuckle in guilty glee over what we call the "Jim-chicken" incident. My neighbor's husband had an old school friend named Jim, who descended upon them periodically for weekend visits. He ate ravenously but never once paid a compliment to my neighbor or her cooking. Though she had two small children he never brought a sack of candy to them. And when on Monday morning he said good-by, it was simply good-by—period.

One Saturday morning she came running over to our house with a beautiful plump frying chicken and a box of strawberries under her apron. "Look," she panted, "can I keep this chicken and strawberries in your icebox until Monday morning? My husband just phoned that he's coming home with him—and I'm *not* going to have Jim eating half of this chicken while the rest of us eat the wings and the gizzard. I'll just give him hamburger. And I'm *not* going to spend an hour making strawberry shortcake—I'll just get some store cookies." She added defensively, "You know how the guy is—I won't even get a thank-you."

"I know," I agreed heartily as I made room in our icebox for her precious viands.

It isn't that we do for, or give to people *just* to receive voluble thanks. But no thanks at all gives us a feeling of "what's the use?" which chills any joy in doing or giving.

I wonder if God doesn't have this same chilled

what's-the-use feeling about many of us. For we pray with such earnest entreaty for His gifts and then when, with a smile, He puts them in our hands and says, "Here you are, my child," we go hurrying on our way without even tossing back over our shoulder a "Thank you, God."

Surely He must have felt the lack of the music of gratitude in the hearts of the suppliants, the receivers.

During this month of November, one day out of the three hundred and sixty-five is set aside for our giving thanks for our benefits and blessings. But even on that day, packed as it is with football games and breakfast before and cocktails after, and letting out the dining table to the utmost for the turkey dinner, how many of us find time for any giving of thanks? Besides, we are so out of the habit of saying prayers of gratitude. Hearts can become as rusty at producing the music of gratitude as fingers can at producing music on the piano. What is that old saying?—something about the favor which is done more than once, becoming not a favor, but something we expect and accept as our due. Not only that but the more favors we receive from heaven the more we expect. Who are the greatest grumblers in life? Usually the people who have the least to grumble about. It has always amazed me that the men and women who have been given so much in talent and worldly goods not only accept these gifts as their due but harp because they are not given more.

The world needs more of the music of gratitude. It is right that we mothers should be diligent and emphatic in teaching thank-you manners to our children. "Now be sure and tell Mrs. Brown that you enjoyed the party and thank her for asking you." But the greater gratitude toward the greatest Giver should be even more forcibly stressed.

Oh, I know that, as children, they won't be too receptive. They might even be ashamed of you. (In my young days I was ashamed of my more devout elders)

. . .Standing at the bus station one night with my two youngest boys, a deformed hunchback hobbled past us. I said, "I never see someone like that without saying a prayer of thanks that you children are all straight and sound and—" Before I could finish the sentence my thirteen-year-old said, "Oh mother!" with vehement disgust. But in later years he may remember (just as my grandmother's remembered prayers come to my lips) when he thanks God for his children that are born, straight of limb and sound of mind. . .

And who could blame God for staying His hand if, for benefits received, He heard not even a faint sound of the music of gratitude in our hearts? So that He, even as my disgruntled neighbor, would be tempted to hold back the equivalent of chicken and strawberry shortcake, and gave us hamburger and store cookies instead?

CHAPTER 9

Let's Look at the Uninhibited

May 1949

One day last week an old school friend telephoned to ask if I'd run down to lunch with some of our old crowd—"Irene Blank is in town." She added with a dry little laugh, "We'll get a chance to see the Great Uninhibited."

"I wouldn't miss it," I said.

Let's see, I mused as I fumbled for a pair of stockings without a run. It's been thirteen—no, fourteen years since Irene visited her home town and lunched with a few of us she had gone to school with. Memories of it still rankled.

I supposed we had looked a rather sorry lot—all except Irene with her bland assurance and her casually expensive clothes. Irene, with her successful career on the coast and her "living her own life" with no regard for conventions or inhibitions. Irene, who didn't want the tedium and chores of marriage but wanted its pleasures without a wedding ring. At the luncheon table fourteen years ago she had talked both freely and casually about her affairs—"Great Romances," she called them.

And I must confess that to her listeners, who were bogged down with small children and unbalanced budgets, "Great Romances" had a more glamorous sound than washing diapers and patching overall knees. I remember that I was ashamed of my hands because I had used a soap powder warranted to remove grease from kitchen walls and it had all but removed my hands as well.

But now, I thought, as I waited for the downtown bus, I'm older and—I hope—wiser. The bus passenger next to me was turning the pages of the morning paper and my eye lighted on a picture of a young engineering graduate who had received some special honor. The young man was the son of an oil man we will call Thornton White. Thornton and his wife had been divorced when their two sons were very small and the mother was given custody of the children.

Thornton had gone his gay, philandering way ever since. His business keeps him traveling through two or three of our western States. He is more than casual—he is quick cocky about having a "sweetie" in practically every town he tarries in. I've heard him say, "I can't help being the way I am—the Lord made me this way." (What queer things the Lord gets credit for!)

So now Thornton's son was graduating with high honors. But Thornton would have no part in it, because both sons are so bitter toward him they do not even speak. I couldn't help wondering if any of Thornton's philandering experiences could make up for the paternal pride and satisfaction he might have felt had he been there to drop his hand on his boy's shoulder and say, "Congratulations son!". . .

At the luncheon table in a downtown restaurant I shook hands with three old school friends—and Irene. My first thought was that the passing of years plays no favorites. Irene looked exactly fourteen years older than when I had seen her last.

My second thought was that life evens things out pretty well. Women in their thirties often look pretty bedraggled with the bearing of, the caring for children, yet, in their late forties, seem to draw a long and satisfying breath and take on a sort of "afterglow."

So that though, as the luncheon progressed, Irene talked with her same colossal contempt for our circumscribed lives, it fell a little flat. For Alice, the mother of five, was telling that her youngest, who'd had a frightening bout with polio five years ago, could now walk without a crutch. Mary told that her first grandchild had been named after her. Becky ate with one eye on the clock; she was to meet her husband at a travel bureau and plan a vacation. Somehow the glamour of Irene's Great Romances seemed a little thin.

I looked at her and I thought, there sits a psychologist's dream of a uninhibited woman. . .And somewhere in this state or the next—with one of his "sweeties," perhaps—is Thornton White, who has never thrust any frustration deep into his unconscious. . .And so what? Are either of them any happier than those of us who belong to the great mess of the Inhibited? No, they weren't. And have either of them contributed to the happiness of the ones their lives have touched? Quite the contrary.

Here were two people who thought they could get the pleasure of sex without making daily, even hourly payments. They are like the spoiled child who picks the raisins out of the bun and throws the more tasteless bread away. He even thinks he is getting the best of it. But later he is bound to feel the lack of nourishment.

The Irenes and Thorntons may think they have had the best of it in getting sex experience without earning it by the chores and worries—even tedium—of marriage. But they have cheated themselves. For sex loses all depth in sacredness and significance if it is reduced to animal level.

For some two-thousand years mankind has sought and has succeeded in wrapping it in the same package with fidelity, tenderness, toil, responsibility, mutual interests—all the things that go with the married state.

Again, I looked at Irene and her bland assurance. But do you have it when you waken in the middle of a dark night? And what about you and the Thorntons of the world when you get past fifty to the sit-by-the-fire state? Who will you have to look back with you to first chapters, to look ahead with you to the coming ones? What about your "the last of life of which the first was made"? What now, Irene? What now, Thornton?

CHAPTER 10

Give Us Parents
a Break

October 1949

Every so often an extremely pat slogan is coined. Whereupon the public accepts it as a bit of gospel and bandies it about with relish. Such a slogan is the one which you and I have heard often in the last few years, "There are no delinquent children; there are only delinquent parents."

I was so impressed by it that I started to write a story using that profound idea as a theme. But, even as I tried to work out the story, I began to doubt the truth of the slogan.

For I remembered my mother saying vehemently (though my mother was a gentle-spoken woman and not given to vehemence), "It's so easy to blame the parents, particularly the mother, every time a son or daughter goes wrong. Yet a tree can't be blamed if one branch grows crooked."

I reasoned on. If it is true that parents are to blame for every child's delinquency, either temporary or permanent, then how can we explain the families with four or five exemplary children and the one "black sheep"? The parents gave the black sheep the same

39

training, the same love as the others, didn't they? Could we call these parents *delinquent*?

About this time an incident happened on our block which gave me a pause.

We live near the big, tree-shadowed city park where, in the summer, band concerts are held nightly. Hundreds of cars are left while the occupants sit in front of the bandstand, listening to the music and watching the interplay of colors on the fountain. The police tell me that for years they have had trouble with boys "prowling" the parked cars, which is police vernacular for stealing anything out of or off of them.

Two boys in our neighborhood were caught at this one night by a policeman. One boy, whom we will call Homer, came from a very strict Swedish home. Homer's parents never allowed him free time, either by day or evening. They always had to know where he was, who he was with and what he was doing.

The other boy, whom we will call Johnny, came from a home where discipline was much more lax. His mother, of necessity, held down a government job. She was a good mother—the kind who wearily repowdered her face to go to school entertainments, who would spend her lunch hour shopping for a First Communion outfit. But, because she was gone all day, she had to put her children on trust.

And here it was her Johnny, whose mother trusted him to do right, and Homer, whose parents kept him under strict surveillance, who went into cahoots on the exciting project of pitting their cunning against the law.

What I want to bring out is that if Homer, alone, had got into this scrape everyone would have said, "Well, no wonder! His parents can blame themselves for acting like jailers. The kids *had* to break over." If Johnny had been in it alone, we would have said, "Well, no wonder! Any kid that can come and go whenever he feels like it and no questions asked, is bound to get into trouble."

Still being doubtful and curious, I spent several days in the juvenile court listening to the cases which came up, talking to social workers and probation officers. It seemed to me that, with but few exceptions, their whole attitude was that of excusing the guilt of young culprits. Social workers turned in reports of the sad conditions at home, and the lack of a playground near it.

Never once did I hear one of the court workers say in essence to the guilty boy or girl, "Look here, why did *you* do this? You know better. Even though the breaks are against you, you must still accept the blame, the reasonability for your own actions. You can tell right from wrong. You have free will."

No, the attitude was, "What can we expect from these children?" So that the delinquents' attitude swiftly mirrored it and beamed, "We aren't to blame. Our family, the whole world is to blame."

It is an unhealthy attitude.

It is true that much of our juvenile delinquency comes from broken homes and the young ones being bruited about. It is true, too, that often the children of delinquent parents turn out to be upright men and women because they had in their soul strong and resilient fiber.

And it is true, too, that many a *good* parent spends years—or even a lifetime—aching over and praying for an erring son or daughter. It is hard for parents and for the critical world to realize that a child is not merely the sum of his parents or the product of his environment and training. He has an identity of his own, even as every dahlia, every colt, every diamond has. And just as some children are born color blind or tone deaf so do we have pathological personalities (not many, thank God!) who are utterly incapable of telling right from wrong. Biologists call this unpredictable variation from the normal a "sport." The zoological term is a "variant."

"There are no delinquent children; there are only delinquent parents." This is but a half-truth.

So before you condemn the parents for the misdemeanors of their child, think.

Especially if you are a parent.

CHAPTER 11

Women, Gainfully Employed

September 1950

It has always seemed ironical to me that statistics list only those women who work *outside* the home as "Gainfully Employed." But what about the women who work inside the home, stretching the budget dollar in casserole meals, in making over dresses for growing daughters, in "doing up" the living room curtains—who, in short, save money which would otherwise be paid out? Aren't they, too, *gainfully* employed?

Carla McGrew is one of the Gainfully Employed because she sells real estate. The McGrews have three growing children. When Carla started, she explained, "I can drive the children to school in the mornings and bring them home, too."

Theoretically it sounded as though she could neatly combine being a wife, mother and successful career woman. But the desires of house-hunting clients can't be fitted into school hours. And Carla has to be on hand when houses are kept open for showing on Sundays.

The last time I saw Carla she was hurriedly buying two cotton formals for her fifteen-year-old Betty. "Imagine," Carla said ruefully, "paying $22.95 for a cotton dress. I could buy the material for a few dollars and whip one up in an afternoon if I weren't trotting people around to look at houses."

"But you're doing pretty well, aren't you, Carla?"

"I've sold three houses this month," she said proudly. "Of course, though we have more money coming in— there's more going out. I have to keep up my car, and spend more for clothes than if I were at home. Mac and I have to entertain at the club because I never know when I'll be tied up with a deal. And our grocery bill is twice as high as it would be if I were home to cut corners. But I can give the children advantages. We've had the boys at camp all summer, and Betty's been taking a drama course."

Then there is Janey Field. Jack Field teaches in the same school with Carla's husband. The Fields have four children, and none too much income. Although Janey herself has a teacher's certificate, she decided her family would be as well off—if not better—if she gave her time and energy to "making do" with her husband's salary, rather than supplementing it.

Janey will hold up for your inspection a small, blue, double-breasted coat. "I copied one I saw downtown— it was twenty-two dollars—and I made this out of an old one of my mother's." When Janey and her husband entertain, Janey cooks the meal. When the bathroom needs painting she gets out the ladder and paint buckets and does it herself. She makes the colorful slip-covers, which get so much wear and tear from children and dogs, that they last only a few years.

Isn't Janey every whit as gainfully employed in saving dollars that would go to a department store, to the club, to a painter, to a decorating company, as if she toiled for someone else beside her family?

More than this, there are the intangibles which statistics have no way of reckoning. It would be interesting to know how many husbands prefer having wives and cooking smells meet them at the door, instead of wives returning from work with them—or even later. (The women of my mother's generation always said with a knowing twinkle, "A good wife is one who gets her hat off before her husband comes home.")

Nor can statistics ever show the number of children who feel a loss and lack at returning home from school to unlock the door of an empty house, or to find only a paid housekeeper who is not at all interested in their spelling test at school. Of children who wistfully envy other children the dogs trailing at their heels, but who are constantly told, "How could you have a dog when there's no one home through the day to take care of it?"

I am not saying a woman should *never* work outside the home. Though, when there are young children, I think there are only two legitimate reasons why a woman should. First, if she is so devoid of homemaking instincts that the routine and drudgery is anathema to her. Then she merely makes herself and everyone around her unhappy. These women, fortunately for husband and children, are the exception.

Second, necessity. Sickness, which entails specialists' and hospital bills; a husband out of work; the extra burden of taking care of parents. Many women are pushed grimly out of the home in order to hold the home together. There is no arguing with necessity. Her children, with children's instinct, recognize it as such and adapt themselves to it.

It's true that mothers who work can give to the family what Carla called "advantages"—the drama course for a daughter, summer camps for the boys—which the one-salaried family often can not. I have noticed, too, that working mothers are apt to be more indulgent with their children than stay-at-home mothers. It may be an unconscious guilty desire—these gifts of new bicycles and formals—to make up for the long absences away from them.

So it would be well for all mothers who, at times, look wistfully at the Gainfully Employed women, to consider well that word "gainfully." To realize that, as Carla said, more money comes in—but more goes out. And that a penny (or a dollar) saved is still a penny (or a dollar) earned.

But even more important is that the "advantages" a stay-at-home mother gives her family more than compensate for the advantages of the Carlas. The homemaking woman is the hub of the wheel, the salver of bruised fingers and feelings, the fillers of stomachs and lack.

She, too, is quite *gainfully* employed.

CHAPTER 12

Thoughts While Waiting for a Telephone Call

October 1950

All morning I have been listening for a call from the hospital. The woman who has been my steadfast friend for some twenty-five years is being operated on. Her husband promised to let me know the outcome promptly. Of course, the haunting questioning is, Will they find the growth benign or malignant?

My thoughts keep going back to our talk three days ago when she was packing to go to the hospital. (Her surgeon wanted her there three days before the operation.)

I went running over with my best housecoat for her to try on. But the sleeves were too short, she decided. "What have I got that you need?" I asked. As I said it, I thought of the many times we had said those words to each other. All through the years we have given each other sympathy, a pair of hose, advice, cold shots, bucking up, a useful kitchen gadget, scoldings. Use when needed.

Who was it who said, "You are rich if you have one friend"? And someone else, "A friend is one who knows all your faults and still loves you."

For though this friend of mine is a writer and we talk over writing plans and criticize each other's work and say frankly, "That's corny," yet our friendship is rooted in the give and take of living with its nagging perplexities, its few little triumphs, its staggering bereavements.

And so that morning while we shakily folded garments and put them in her grip, she told me what the doctor had said, told me how the night before she had waited till after her husband had dinner and listened to the ball game by radio before she told him. She added, "I'm not afraid of the operation. You and I have talked about pain—we can both stand that. And I'm not afraid to die—I've talked that over with God before. But it's the long, long months of pain and slow decay that fill me with terror. I don't know whether I have that kind of courage or not."

I said soberly, "Courage doesn't come in big chunks. You ask for it when you need it—for the hour or even the minute to carry you through—and you get it."

We were interrupted several times by friends telephoning to "cheer her up." At the end of one conversation she smiled wryly, "All of them are saying, 'Just don't even think that it will be the worst. Just have Faith that everything will be all right.' Can you get comfort out of that kind of thinking?"

"No. Whenever I don't know what the outcome will be. I always ask myself, 'What is the worst that can happen?' And then face the worst. You can't turn your back on it—at least, I can't—"

"I can't either," she admitted. "No matter how hard you try, it keeps niggling at your skirts. But you know about that—because you went through this same doubt and torture."

Five years ago our family doctor said to me, as doctors have said to so many women, "There's a sizeable tumor. I can't say whether it's malignant or not. I'll make an appointment for you with Doctor X."

It was four days before I could get an appointment with him.

They were long days and even longer nights. You can cram your days full, but in the long watches of the night, you have to face the spectre and look smack into its dark countenance and say to yourself, "This could be the end." At first there is only the numb feeling of, "It couldn't happen to me." But realism answers, "Yes, it could. You're no exception." You reach out to God in cringing terror. . .and finally He gives you the serenity to say, "If this is Your will, give me the courage and strength."

It is amazing how you view life with different, almost X-ray eyes. Lying awake at night, planning for the protection and guidance of the younger children, I found that the only quality that stood out clean in the folks about me—even the ones I loved—was "goodness." Charm, brilliance, efficiency became blurred.

I remember, too, a poet-lecturer telling of how, during the war, he was captured by the enemy and sentenced to the firing squad. And how, after living with the thought of certain death for two weeks, he somehow escaped. He said, "I am a different man. Never again will I fret over petty, everyday worries. If my laundry is lost, if I don't make train connections, if I miss a meal or two— it doesn't matter."

And, only a few days ago, a young mother of three who had undergone an emergency operation of dubious outcome, said, "I think no one can have the right values in life until he has actually felt Death breathing on his cheek."

When my four days of waiting were up and the specialist turned to me and said, "It isn't malignant," I was so suddenly overwhelmed with gratitude to God that He had stayed the cup. Those three nights of looking death in the face had brought me closer to God, closer to life. I felt a new dedication to living; although, having great human frailties, I am ashamed to say I haven't lived up to that high moment.

I kept waiting for the phone to ring.

She called me once from the hospital before the doctor gave orders that there were to be no phone conversations. She said, "I'm pretty dopey, but my mind is all right—and I feel very serene, a sort of 'Be still and know that I am God.' "

And always selfishness enters into our hopes, fears and prayers. I keep thinking of the innumerable times we walked around the lake in the park—of days when we laughed with such hearty abandon that we could only bump drunkenly into each other; of other days when we walked on weighted feet and sighed more than we talked. Life would lack a real dimension without her.

. . .The telephone call has just come through. That blessed, that beautiful word, "Benign." Deo gratias! I know so well the feeling she will have when she is told, that grateful humility of "Thank you, God, for this reprieve. May I prove worthy of it!"

CHAPTER 13

Slang—a Blessing—a Blemish

June 1951

Coming home one day last week on a crowded, swaying bus my companion and I listened to this slice of conversation between two girls of high school age:

"Hi, Marge. Long time no see."

"Oh hi, Peg. You sure picked yourself off a sunburn."

"You ain't just champing your gums. Hey, what churns in the box?" (Meaning, "What have you in the suit box you're carrying?")

"New dine and dance number. And boy, oh boy, is it out of this world—absolutely. But wait till Pop takes a gander at it. Will he blow his top!"

"You telling me! Mine had baby kangaroos the last time I splurged on a glad rag."

My companion happened to be a French woman who speaks English beautifully and fluently. She turned to me to ask dazedly, "What language are they speaking? I find it unintelligible."

"Pure high school slang," I explained indulgently. "They can carry on for hours like that."

I am sure she would have been even more mystified if she had followed me home. For at the moment my thirteen-year-old son disposes of everything by two

51

descriptive words—neaty and hairy. "A neaty, old picture," means that the movie he has just sat through had a minimum of love-making and a maximum of trigger action. "A hairy, old spelling test," conveys that he probably missed some twenty-eight words out of fifty. "A neaty, old hamburger," means that his sandwich was replete with onion, dill pickle and mustard. "A hairy, old basketball game," tells us that the side he was rooting for lost.

Perhaps her very mystification, her finding our liberal use of slang unintelligible, sharpened my ears in days that followed. And I found that it was not only the thirteen-year-olds, the high school age which relies almost wholly on slangful patter. In the store a gray-haired, middle-aged matron (how perfectly that description fits me) described a lecturer as being out of this world.

Slang has a reason for being. We Americans have always been a lusty people, ever veering away from the prescribed, the hackneyed. Our whole-hearted acceptance of slang really stems from an instinctive desire for freshness and novelty of expression. Often the slang phrase sums up a whole situation briefly, pithily. It would take almost a paragraph to explain what is perfectly clear in, "Mary gave John the gate." or "He packs a powerful wallop."

It is this same seeking of freshness and novelty which keeps our slang expressions constantly changing. *Skidoo, twenty-three* and *beat it* all had their turn and have given way to our present *scram*. It, in turn, has become so threadbare that we could wish it would *scram* and give way to a newer. In my time the word for lovemaking has traveled the same ever-changing road: *spoon, pet, pitching-woo, neck* to the present *smooch*. (Pardon me, a university student corrects me: *warm the form* is the ultra. The latest.)

The general credo of present-day living is toward a more free and easy informality. The average wardrobe today is liberally sprinkled with unconfining housecoats, jeans—and loafers, comfortable to the point of dropping off our heels. The average conversation today sounds school teacherish and stilled without a liberal sprinkling of slang.

But there is a dangerous and insidious side to the using of slang. We come to rely almost wholly upon the newly-coined or the thread-bare expression. And just as its aptness, its pungency enriches our conversation and our writing, so does it banalise and impoverish it. We become sloppy talkers and writers for the slang word is always there within too easy reach. We are comparable to a person who opens her closet door and finds only jeans and shapeless shoes.

Remember that while some slang is crisp and meaningful, much of it is frayed to meaninglessness. Remember that our language is bounteous in itself. The right word can cut like a blade, can soothe like a caress. In everyday living what slang words are fitting substitute for *endearing, anguish, beloved, wean, holy, gritty*? Remember, too, that through centuries our language has been the means of stirring men with hope, conveying heartbreak, revealing to us the Greatest Story and the truths we live by.

So let us keep on using slang, but let us not be beggared by it. Thoughts are real and precious things. Words are the raiment we give them. Let us clothe them in force, poignancy and beauty.

CHAPTER 14

Good Samaritan—1951

September 1951

Now I know how a stranger in a strange land feels. He feels lost and bewildered—yes, and panicky at finding that his native tongue is but gibberish to those about him, even as their language is to him. And I know, too, the wondrous relief of the weary, confused stranger when one person goes out of his way to help him.

For it happened to me the night we arrived in Rome.

Of course, "seeing the Pope" was to be the highlight of my trip to Europe. After visiting my student son in Paris, a young girl and I set out for Rome in a secondhand midget car. Some fifty percent of the cars in France are midgets because gasoline costs about seventy cents a gallon and they, quoting road advertisements, have "the appetite of a bird."

We were five days on the road between Paris and Rome. For our little Fiat may have had the appetite of a bird—but not its swiftness. It wound its way through French countryside, picturesque as postcards, chugged painfully up mountains that seemed steeper than our Rockies, felt its impeded way through little towns and big cities where pedestrians saunter blithely in the streets and everyone from five to eighty rides bicycles. It purred along the Mediterranean, bluer even than poets have pictured it.

In France we managed fairly well at ordering meals and renting rooms. Jane has lived eight months in Paris, and I'd had a month there to furbish up my schoolroom French—though my manhandling of tenses must both amaze and amuse my listeners.

But we spoke no Italian.

As Jane drove, I sat beside her with our book of conversational Italian. We drilled ourselves on counting, saying "please" and "thank you," and I memorized "We would like a room with two beds." However, we found where we stopped at gas stations, an inn for lunch, or an albergo for the night that our sign language was understood better than our Italian.

Rome is well down the leg of the boot which is Italy.

We planned to reach the Holy City the middle of a Sunday afternoon. A strange town seems less strange in broad daylight. We could get our bearings and hunt for a certain hotel, mentioned in our guide book.

So we planned.

We noticed that Sunday morning, as we made time on Mussolini's good road to Rome, a goodly sprinkling of polissio. Two of them even halted us, but finding us Americanos, who couldn't understand, motioned us on.

But halfway to Rome we were stopped and motioned in beside a Shell Service Station along with other cars, motorcycles and trucks. We didn't know why. No one about us could speak anything but Italian, until a girl in a Denmark car explained in broken English that it was because of an automobile race or timing course from Rome to Provo—"and the road shall be clear because these cars come through—Whoosh!"

That was at eleven.

The first two cars—midgets—to whoosh down the road came about one. Hopefully we waited. The sun was hot. The people gathered there to wait or to watch were friendly but un-understandable. Two o'clock, three—four, and still, at intervals, the numbered cars roared by. We were hot, hungry, head-achy. It was after five when, at last, the policemen let traffic go on.

That was the reason we arrived at Rome long after dark. The reason we became snarled in traffic inside Rome again and again, why traffic police routed us this way and that until we were hopelessly confused and lost and couldn't find our way out of Vatican City and to the center of town, we didn't realize until the next day.

It was the day of the Beatification of Pius X. St. Peter's had just emptied itself of its forty thousand participants. Over twice that many, they told us, had packed the Piazza outside. No wonder the streets were literally packed with pedestrians and traffic. Twice busy traffic officers tried to direct us but their direction weren't clear to us.

Riding beside Jane as she threaded her way through the maze of traffic, or momentarily drove down a more quiet street, I craned my neck for a glimpse of some sort of lodging. Sometimes she stopped while I got out trying to inquire how to get to the center of town. People only shook their heads and hurried on their way.

Finally we saw the sign Albergo on a shabby, formidable building. We were too weary and desperate by now to be choosy, so I went in, mentally rehearsed the Italian for "room for the night—for two." A dour and unfriendly man scowled up at me from behind a desk. A woman, equally unfriendly, sat there knitting. I fumbled out my poor Italian. I will never know whether he didn't want to be bothered with foreigners or if, perhaps, he held some grudge against Americans. But he shook his head grimly—no rooms. He even motioned me out. (This was the only time on our trip that we met anything but helpful courtesy.)

My legs were weak as I went back to the car. I could see that Jane was limp and exhausted. I felt panicky. We couldn't go on like this.

My eyes lightened on two young priests across the street and I hurried over. Did either of them speak English? No. French? Yes, one spoke French. In my stumbling French I explained that we were lost, that we wanted to find a hotel.

He took me by the arm and walked with me across the street and to the car. Never, I'm sure, will I ever feel anything so heartening as his firm grip on my arm.

I suppose he saw that we needed more than directions. He consulted his watch. Later, I realized, that it was close to ten o'clock when seminarians must be inside Vatican City. He called over a man he had been talking to, and delegated him to pilot us safely to a downtown hotel. The priest's emissary not only guided us through miles of packed streets but, at the hotel, went in and arranged for our room.

We wanted to pay him. We tried to give him taxi fare back. He wouldn't take so much as lira. Father had sent him and he wanted no payment.

In a way it seems appropriate that a priest should be the first to befriend us in the Holy City. A priest who will always be unknown for in the confusion no one asked names. But I wish he could know how much it meant to us. We were so weary, so confused. . .

And, in thinking about it, I have made one firm resolve. Whenever a bewildered stranger in my city turns to me for help I will do more than point out directions which he will have trouble following. I will take him or her by the arm and say, "I will help you."

It is the only way I know of showing gratitude to that good Samaritan in his flat priest's hat. And always in my prayers I will remember him.

CHAPTER 15

Take Only a Leaf

March 1952

For more years than I should like to enumerate, it has rankled within me that most business and professional women carry the double load of work outside the home and work within it. Why, I have often raged, can't we women recognize our limitations?

Take unmarried Jane, who works in an advertising office next to unmarried John. Jane—oh, maybe her name is Kathie or Marge—either lives at home with her folks or keeps up her own apartment. John's setup is the same.

If Jane lives with her family she has probably, during the day, received phone calls from home. Would she have time on her noon hour to buy some of the yarn on sale? Could she stop at the bakery on her way home for rolls?

At home Jane helps with the dinner (the doctor has told her mother to take it easy) and washes the dishes. She launders her blouse, underwear, stockings; she presses her suit skirt, letting down or taking up a hem. If our Jane lives in an apartment, she must on her way home push through a crowded super market for dinner groceries and sweet rolls for breakfast. She gets her own dinner, does the same laundering and sewing chores she would do at home, and even works late on a chintz spread for her couch by day, bed by night.

The John who lives at home matches no yarn on his noon hour, and buys no groceries after leaving the office. He reads the paper until dinner is put on the table. If John lives in an apartment he goes out to dinner, after dropping his bundle of shirts and underwear into a laundry chute, and leaving his suit for the cleaner with a reminder that the pockets need mending.

Let's look at Jane (or Kathie or Marge) fifteen years older, married and with three children. Her husband's salary has lagged far behind increased living costs. Now that the children are in school why shouldn't she take her job back to help pay for building that extra room on the house? After all, a two-bedroom house won't do for three kids.

So Jane gets up earlier in order to breakfast the family and get the children off to school. At noon she grabs a malt and package sandwich so as to take her son's boots to the shoe repair shop, and buy a plaid blouse for her daughter. She interrupts her work to phone home to enjoin small Johnny to take his cold medicine, to remind the older daughter to put potatoes in the oven. She streaks home from work to get dinner. The children help, of course: even the husband leaves his radio long enough to wipe dishes. But on balmy Saturday afternoons when husbands are on the golf course, when children are playing or watching baseball. Jane is hanging dripping blankets on the line, washing windows, or giving her teenage daughter a home permanent.

Now let us suppose our Jane (or Kathie or Marge) is widowed. The insurance is not adequate so an outside job is the only answer. Here again a woman differs from a man. When a man's wife dies he doesn't try to be both mother and father. His job has always been the bringing home of bacon for someone else to cook. Perhaps some unattached grandmother or aunt comes into his home; or he hires a housekeeper. But seldom does the widow have help from relatives or a paid housekeeper.

Why do most of us women think we should keep on frying the bacon as well as bringing it home? Because we are inherently homemakers. For countless generations we have tended fires, tucked in blankets, dosed up croupy children. For comparatively few generations have we pounded typewriters, given out lesson assignments, written advertising copy. (Occasionally, yes, you find a woman who happily flees to an office or school room so she can pay out the bulk of her salary to someone else to do the housework she loathes.)

So through the years I have come to realize that the working woman must indulge her true feminine side. One successful woman realtor, after winding up a tough deal, always hies herself to a beauty shop and then buys a glamorous hat. Psychologists predict dire things for the career woman who squelches her woman cravings.

So I don't suggest that working women become men in skirts.

But it is a mistake for us to think we can carry full time housekeeping along with a job. To begin with, the average woman hasn't robust enough health for the double burden. She becomes frazzled and fatigued and complaining until she is no treat in office or home. And, because her primary aim in working is to do more for her family, she is defeating her purpose if, in adding extra money to the home, she subtracts from its serenity, zest, or shared laughter.

We should, like our husbands and brothers, realize our limitations. This means sloughing off all unnecessary fripperies while still holding to the spirit of home life; putting away linen napkins for paper ones, buying the birthday cake instead of baking it, simplifying Sunday dinners and entertaining.

And we should strive for a more equal distribution of the work in the home. This generation, I believe, does not have the line so sharply defined as to what is women's work, what is men's. I think of the young working couples I know where the husband bathes the baby, whips up pancakes, runs the vacuum sweeper. My son-in-law is not above taking two toddlers to the barber shop with him so as to give their mother a nap. The young husband next door takes their two-year-old to a softball game while his wife works over the bills she gets out for a doctor each month. This generation of husbands seems more willing to recognize that when the wife helps in bringing home bacon he can help with the frying.

In short, when a woman holds a man's job in a man's world she can well take a leaf from a man's book. Not the whole book, for a man's rules will never spell wholeness or happiness for her. Just take that leaf which says, "You can't be all things at all times."

CHAPTER 16

Visitors Welcome

February 1953

It is so easy for any of us to rally with swift sympathy and generosity when catastrophe hits someone we know. We rush in, all anxiety to help. And then, our sympathy and generosity spent, it is so easy for us to go our busy way forgetting that the unfortunate one may still need us—perhaps more than he did at first.

Do you remember how during the war (the war we *called* a war, that is) we were all anxiety to do for the sick and wounded in Veterans' Hospitals? We put on entertainments, we baked cookies for them, we visited at their bedsides. But when the war was over (or so we thought), all too many of us with our full and busy lives found it easy to forget how time drags in hospital wards for the boys and men whose lives are neither full nor busy.

Yet our government hospitals are still full of the maimed, the sick, the deranged from three wars.

Last month in an article on visiting the sick, I suggested that often a visitor's absence is more welcome than his presence. But that applies only to the person who is ill briefly. It doesn't apply to anyone with a long-time illness. And certainly not to the inmates of Veterans' Hospitals.

For so many of them—the neurological, multiple sclerosis, paraplegic cases—are in for years, even a lifetime of therapy. Many veterans of World War I, gray-haired, spiritless, are still shuffling drearily through corridors, almost forgotten by the world outside. It is visitors who break the bleak monotony of their days and keep them from feeling that they are indeed Forgotten Men.

And then there are the men in "Locked Wards," who desperately need the interest and understanding of those on the outside. Perhaps you feel, even as I did before I started going to "Eleven North," an inadequate feeling of, "Oh, I wouldn't be any good around mental cases." But you would. You would need only common sense and a sincere desire to help.

Monday night is party night in the Locked Ward of our Veterans' Hospital. A friend of mine acts as hostess every week. Carrying a portable record player, dance records, playing cards, two or three of us older women, with some pretty young girls in tow, pass through the heavy doors, unlocked by attendants, and into the recreation room where from twenty to thirty men and boys are waiting. We dance with those who want to dance; we play cards or visit with those who don't. In this case it's the woman who must say, "Come on, let's dance," or "How about a game of cribbage?" because these mental cases are apt to be shy, aloof. At the start, that is.

And I am sure that you would be amazed, even as I, that after that first small shock of keys clanking in heavy doors, you forget that these men about you are "different." But, then, as one of them put it, "we aren't crazy all the way through. We just got a quirk or two to iron out."

At these Monday night parties in the Locked Ward it is the young, nimble-footed girls the boys like to dance with. They treat them with wondrous courtesy. No mother of a girl need worry about her daughter who gives an evening to lift the spirits of sick soldiers.

Yet the boys in this ward or any ward also like the

homey touch of the older women who say, "Why, I've got a boy just your age." It is the older woman to whom they show pictures of the family; the older woman they ask to write letters for them.

And how mail is watched for by these men in bed or in bathrobes and flapping slippers! A man slumped in despairing apathy brightens when the nurse hands him a letter or card. If you have a relative or friend within those brick walls, keep writing to him. Clip cartoons that will give him a chuckle. Send snap shots.

And how gifts are cherished! The old reliable ones— cigarettes, candy or cookies (preferably homemade), stationery, socks, T-shirts. They like gifts that help pass time away—puzzles or a canasta set. Above all, they like gifts they can share with their ward mates—that box of homemade cookies, or the paper-backed books to pass around. . .The brother of a T.B. patient carted to the hospital an antelope he had killed. The cook served it several times to the whole T.B. ward. And each time that boy strutted happily with the proud satisfaction of, "I've done something for someone else.". . .I know a schoolteacher with a paraplegic nephew in a smaller ward with three other bedridden men. Each Sunday she bakes a pie and takes it out to them. They are like children, watching the clock all day, guessing among themselves as to what kind of a pie it will be this time.

I know that many who are reading this are miles from cities where government hospitals are located. But I know, too, that in smaller towns and outlying districts many people have more conscience about the veteran's needs than we have who are within a bus ride of them. The out-of-towners can and do keep in touch with the Red Cross and so keep their gifts pouring in.

But do any of us have enough conscience? The drama, the glamour of doing for our "brave boys" in wartime has somehow dimmed. I know it is trite to quote, "They gave so much; we should give a little in return." But it is still true. They did: and we should.

Hospital builders, hospital staffs strive valiantly to replace institutional coldness with the homey touch. But in spite of bright curtains, easy chairs, radios, men's wards are still dreary things. The warmth, the understanding, the cheer must come from the outside. Visitors welcome. I keep remembering the boy who said, "When we're alone we sit and brood. You look around and see all the other guys brooding, too. Then all at once in comes a few skirts and—by golly!—the whole world picks up."

CHAPTER 17

Long Range Kindness

March 1953

Martha's life these days is all work and worry. She is beginning to be resentful and defensive. Folks say to me, "You ought to tell her why no woman will stay with her little girl while she works, why all her friends have dropped off, why every man who shows interest in her does a quick fadeout. Martha would take it better from you than anyone else."

But I cringe at the thought of hurting Martha who is only twenty-nine, and whom I have known and loved for years. It would be easier if she weren't kind and gentle, if she hadn't dedicated herself to being a good mother to her small Sheila who was born several months after Martha's husband was killed in an automobile accident.

Sheila is four now. When you first see her, with her auburn curls and blue eyes, your heart warms with the thought, "What an adorable child!" But after ten minutes of Sheila's interrupting every conversation, her demanding the spotlight, her bullying her mother, you think, "What a brat!"

Once after Martha and Sheila had stopped in, one of our family queried irately, "Is there any law against telling a kid to shut up?"

I answered wearily, "There wasn't when I was raising mine. There wasn't even one against a small swat on a small behind when you were bedeviled beyond endurance."

This is what I would like to say to Martha if—or when—I can summon enough courage:

Martha dear, when Sheila was born you said you had to make up to her for not having a father. But you aren't doing it by indulging and spoiling her. You wouldn't go to your office party last week because you said that when you were gone through the day you owed it to Sheila to spend all your evenings and holidays with her. Why do you? Other women have to work to support a child or children, and still have a life of their own without cheating their one or more children. It's healthy for a child to feel he can depend on a parent; but un-healthy to feel he owns a parent.

Your very kindness has made Sheila into a demanding little virago. You can't go on and on, always hunting a new housekeeper to take care of her. You can't go on and on, leaving the house each morning, torn and harried by her clinging to you and screaming.

And you condemn your friends for falling off. You were both hurt and furious when the Smiths asked you out to dinner—and then pointedly suggested that you leave Sheila at home. But really, honey, even though our family is *used* to the din and hubbub of children, when Sheila is at the table none of us knows whether he's eating baled hay or pot roast. Not with Sheila yelling out her temper because she wants her milk in a glass goblet, or whining when you urge her to clean up her plate. Not with her squirming down from the table and mauling the kittens and turning the dials of the T.V. set and losing the pegs off the cribbage board.

Through it all you reason and plead with her. There are times when patience becomes a vice.

But oh, Martha, your most woeful mistake is letting

Sheila crowd out and scare off the men in your life. Remember that nice man in the office next to yours who asked you to have dinner with him? And how he brought Sheila a doll and candy?

But when the babysitter came Sheila realized you were leaving her, and went into such a jealous rage that she threw the doll down and tramped on it and dumped the candy down the register. You went out distraught, ate a hurried dinner, passed up a show so as to get back to Sheila.

Is it any wonder you've never heard from him again?

Now don't say defensively that men aren't interested in a woman with a child. That isn't fair. Most any man, who loves a woman, would gladly take on the extra responsibility of a ready-made son or daughter. It's being done all the time. But no man wants a jealous little tartar forever coming between him and his wife.

You need a husband, Martha. You say you only want to make a happy home for Sheila. But it's only half a home without a man in it. You want and need a husband because you are more of a homemaker than a career woman. And Sheila, even as any child, needs a father for a normal growing up.

When adoption agencies ruled that a woman without a husband couldn't take a child it was wisdom born of long-tested experience.

So, Martha, think of the years ahead. And of the awful disfavor to Sheila to let her think the world revolves around her. The spoiled brats of the world are the unhappy adults. You hear parents say, "I want to do all I can for my children because life will be hard for them later." But it will be far harder if they meet it coddled, and pampered and undisciplined.

It sounds strange, child, to advise you to be more selfish, more impatient, more stubborn. When you're tired in the evenings say to Sheila, "I'll tell you one story; then I want to take a bath and read in bed." When she constantly interrupts conversation, an impatient,

"Either keep still or go upstairs," would be more salutary than lengthy reasoning. When she refuses to eat her dinner but later wants cookies, match her stubbornness with your own. It sounds strange to say that unkindness now will be kindness in the long run."

. . .Yes, unkindness is often kind-ness in the long run. So surely I would be doing Martha a kindness to tell her unkind truths now. But I wonder if I'll ever have the courage. . .

CHAPTER 18

I'm Moving in with My Son's Family

August 1953

Grandma Connor took the lilacs from me and said, "Come out in the kitchen and we'll have a cup of tea." She closed the old-fashioned, narrow window against the noisy filling station on one side and bottling works on the other. I watched her bustling about with the alert and prideful hospitality of a woman in her own home. Yet, next week she must walk out of it and into the home of her son's family!

While riding over with Alice Connor and listening to her worries over Grandma Connor's moving in with them, I must confess that my sympathies had been all for the daughter or daughter-in-law who must adjust to an elderly grandma in the home. But when the old lady poured tea and said shakily, "I'm pretty broken up over leaving my own place here," I realized with a pang what this uprooting meant.

For in her old home, where she had brought up a family, she was an individual—not just Grandma or Ed's mother or Alice's mother-in-law. She was moving into another woman's home. It is the mover-in who must always make the harsher adjustments.

I could only murmur inanely, "I'm sure you can work

71

it out."

I found that she, too, was haunted by certain horrible examples. She spilled them out over our tea. There was Mary Daly who had moved in with her son. Mary, overly anxious not to be a burden, had gradually been turned into a full-time cook, cleaning woman, dishwasher and babysitter in the home. "She never even had time to come to our Guild meetings. She worked harder raising her grandchildren than she did her own—and precious little thanks she got for it!"

"But Alice and Ed want you to have it easy," I said, quoting Alice. "You needn't worry—"

"But I don't want to be treated like a senile idiot, either. There was poor Ollie Tracy—you remember her, Mrs. Frank Tracy? She moved in with her daughter. They shoved her off in her room. She couldn't sew or cook—or even mop—to suit them. Well I saw Ollie turn into a whining invalid. I suppose it was the only way the poor thing could get a little attention—"

. . .And a sad attempt, I remembered sadly. For Mrs. Frank Tracy ended her days in a convalescent home. . .

"Ed's family don't *need* me," my hostess went on unhappily. "But I'm not old enough to be put on the shelf. The trouble nowadays is that old women live too long. Life is no gift when you're no longer useful."

I have often thought the same thing. Medical science has done oldsters a dubious favor in prolonging their lives long after their capabilities have decreased. And doesn't it seem ironical that while the medical world has lengthened the lifespan, the economic world has shortened the work span? God help the man or woman over fifty who tries to get a job in a big organization these days!

"But, Grandma Connor, you're still a very capable woman in your own right."

"Indeed I am," she said proudly, "in my own home. I could keep boarders if this wasn't such a ratty part of town that I'd only get riff-raff I'd be afraid to have under my roof. I'm a good cook, but my ways aren't Alice's. And I still clean with a broom and the kind of a mop you wring out yourself. I'm too old to learn how to use all those new-fangled gadgets on a vacuum, or automatic thises and thats."

"Don't say that," I scolded. "If Alice's fourteen-year-old can use them, you certainly can. What else are you troubled about?"

"Of being an old nuisance every morning. I have to be sick to stay in bed after six—and I get sick if I don't have coffee by six-thirty. I like to go to early Mass. But they won't want me clattering around before they're up. And another thing," she added ruefully, "I'm used to the morning paper being my paper—not waiting till everyone else has pulled it to pieces."

"What else?" I prodded.

"I'll miss my old cronies dropping in for a cup of tea now and then. But, heavens, we old biddies will be no treat for Alice and the children—"

"And Alice and the children will be no treat to you and your friends," I amended. "I guess that's one of the hardest lessons anyone has to learn, remember the jolt it was when one of my boys had company and said to me, 'Hey, Mom, can't you fade?' And on the other hand, my fifteen-year-old looks amazed when I say to him, 'Run along now—Mrs. Lane and I want to talk, and you cramp our style.'"

She smiled at that. She admitted further, "Yes, and it's hard for me to keep my mouth shut about the way children are brought up these days."

"I know. I have to watch myself so I won't say to a son or daughter-in-law, 'What that kid needs is a good clout.'"

. . ."What else are you worried about?"

"About paying my way. I'm not destitute. I have some pension—not much, because they took out for my having a home, and now they'll deduct the little rent I'll get for this place. I'd feel better if I were contributing something. But Ed—bless his heart!—won't let me mention it."

I thought, yes, Ed—bless his well-meaning heart!—in a desire to be magnanimous, was overlooking his mother's pride and independence.

"Of course, I'll be extra expense, extra trouble, extra nuisance," she burst out despairingly. "All my life I've been the Queen Bee in my own home. How am I ever going to keep from being such a thorn in their sides that every time I cough they'll hope I'm getting pneumonia?" Her laugh choked in her throat, her face worked.

At that, Ed's wife, Alice, opened the front door and, hearing voices, came out into the kitchen.

CHAPTER 19

Not a Baby,
Not a Man

May 1954

Several mornings ago our paper carried a story on juvenile delinquency and its alarming increase in our city. Why, challenged the reporter, with all our recreational youth programs, our community centers, our nine-o'clock curfew law, had vandalism, purse-snatching, traffic violations, robbery—even murder—increased?

And I can well imagine every parent of growing children uneasily asking himself, "What can we do about it? How can we guide our own safely through the worrying years from eleven to eighteen?"

I have five sons; the youngest is now sixteen. For some eighteen years our house and yard have been overrun with boys—good ones, bad ones, in-between ones. Although I do not claim to be an expert, but because of being surrounded by boys all these years, I think I know some of the whys for this present-day increase in delinquency. I am speaking only of boys brought up in a city because that is the problem I am closest to.

In the first place, these boys haven't enough to keep them busy. They don't have chores thrust on them at an early age. To be sure, city boys get jobs—part-time when attending school—but while that solves one problem, it is apt to pose more. For these jobs of ushering at shows, working at drive-ins or drugstores, involve late-at-night hours, the making of undesirable money to spend.

Conditions in most cities have worsened for boys these last years. Sixteen or eighteen years ago our town was comfortably spread out, and boys had vacant lots for baseball games or football scrimmage. Now these lots are solidly built up; rendezvous must be held on street corners or in the drugstore or alley.

And today is a "car" age. Even before our boys reach the legal age for obtaining a car license, their hands itch to get hold of a wheel. Today the talk I overhear in our kitchen is all of "hotrods." I know so-called "nice" boys who are on probation for stealing cars. I asked one of them, "Timmy, whatever possessed you to take that car?" He squirmed ashamedly, "Oh, I guess I just wanted to see what it would do if I really opened it up. I figured I could put it back before they caught me."

Our older sons came up through the Depression and near-depression years. They, and all their friends, sensed that it was useless to demand new sport jackets and an allowance. Teenage boys today have come up when money in the average family was more plentiful, but they have come up under the cloud of war unrest. Our sixteen-year-olds are already anticipating Uncle Sam's hand on their shoulders. It gives them a certain "What's the use?" cynicism about earnest work at school or taking job that might lead to a better one later. As my son says, "When you know the Army is going to grab you, you want to get all the kicks you can beforehand."

But I am convinced that the worst contributing factor to today's muddled-up adolescence is the soft, shilly-shallying attitude we have taken toward it. All this spotlighting, this great to-do of sympathy for the poor misunderstood youth! Excuses for his running amok have been practically put on his own lips. We parents, educators, yes, even court workers, have been so ready to blame circumstances or someone else for his misdemeanors that the culprit feels himself blameless. We have striven so mightily to do right by our young that we have done wrong by them.

And we have turned out a crop of adolescents who are selfish, inconsiderate, ungrateful, demanding. Of all the parents I know, I can name none who are too strict. I can name plenty, myself included, who are too lenient.

Yet, it isn't enough to see the whys. What can parents do, you ask, to decrease delinquency? Well, if there is any pat solution I wish I knew it.

But because the situation is costing you and me hectored days and sleepless nights, it is up to us to do both more—and less. To give them more of our time, more of ourselves, more surveillance, more ideals; and less humoring, less material things, less letting them feel all-important.

Sometimes I envy rural families of several decades ago when there was more family participation; when whole families from grandma down to the new baby, set off in the wagon or surrey to a box-supper or a Sunday visit with neighbors. It made for family "oneness" with men of all ages playing horse-shoes, with old women and young girls talking trousseaux and layettes.

Yet, we can and should work at a modern-day facsimile of it. As a family we can go to church bingo parties, to movies, on all-day picnics. For the family and home is still the most solid bulwark against our children getting into trouble outside the home.

We should keep them in the home and off the streets as much as we can. Even if it means sacrifice on the parents' part—giving over the TV and the living room to boys watching two-gun Westerns. The gang instinct is strong in even small boys. It is better to sacrifice the flower beds in the back yard for their digging of a cave—a cave they call their "club house"—than to have them ganging up out of sight.

With juvenile delinquency rampant, our children need sharper oversight. "Where are you going? Whom are you going with? Freddy who? Where does he live? What time will you get in?"...One mother says almost tearfully, "But Donnie gets mad if I ask him questions." ...But haven't we worried too much about our children getting mad at us, their not liking us, and not enough about their lack of consideration, their wanting an independence they haven't earned?

These days it takes a deal of watching, a deal of praying. Praying for the wisdom to guide us and them: praying for the strength to say "no" and stick to it in spite of the injured air or argument. Parenting these days calls for Divine help.

CHAPTER 20

Three Women and a Prayer

July 1954

I want to tell you about an expereince I had. In a way it is a confession story with a two-thirds happy ending.

It started one late summer evening when a young woman (I'll call her Eudora) was taking an older woman, Jane (that isn't her real name, either) and me home from a book review. At the close of it the reviewer had quoted a fitting line from St. Francis of Assisi's prayer, and the words somehow haunted—and reproached me.

Eudora stopped at Jane's house first, that substantial four-bedroom house where Jane, a childless widow, has lived alone since her husband's death years ago. You have to use banal descriptions for Jane; set in her ways, well-fixed, penny-pinching. All the way home she was complaining about how lonely she was, how unfriendly her neighbors were, how none of her old friends ever phoned her anymore—

Neither Eudora nor I offered much to cheer her up. I could imagine how trivial that all sounded to Eudora. For only a month ago she had been humiliatingly jilted.

The pre-jilted Eudora had been a bubbling-over attractive woman with a penchant for pretty hats. She was in her middle thirties, and worked in an advertising firm. For three years she had been "going with" a widower named Howard, with two small children. In those three years Eudora always explained that they couldn't marry until Howard paid off the debts incurred by his wife's long illness; then that they must somehow make arrangements for Howard's mother who was caring for the children.

A half-year ago Howard's firm transferred him to the West Coast. And last month Eudora received word that Howard was married. . .This post-jilted Eudora had sat through the book review, looking drawn and defensive and bitter, and ten years older. Even her auburn hair looked dull and lifeless.

Indeed, we were a sodden trio in that car. I was just plain grumpy. I was tired and frazzled. I felt put-upon. Here, I had writing to do for my livelihood, yet I was the one who was always interrupted, who must remember to bring the milk in out of the heat, and keep the back door shut against the flies. I was the one to get up at night to let the dog out. I saw no chance of a vacation for myself—yet all summer long hadn't vacationers descended on me from trains and buses and cars and planes? . . .Yes, I was indulging in a fine spell of self-pity.

Jane drew from her purse a clanking chunk of keys. "What on earth do you use all those keys for?" Eudora challenged.

Jane defended plaintively, "Remember, I'm all alone. I have to lock the front door, and then the vestibule door. And my fur coat closet, and my cedar chest—and, of course, my silver drawer. You never can tell about cleaning women—"

What a fear-filled, locked-up existence!

And then, because I couldn't get that quote from St. Francis out of my mind, I said, "You know what we three cross-grained women ought to do? We ought to try to change ourselves and our lives by following the prayer of St. Francis for a month. Come on, let's do it. We'll be meeting in a month at the next book review. Let's see how it works."

"I've got to try something," Eudora murmured desolately. Jane sounded a little dubious. "Well, I'll try." We watched Jane until she was safely inside her well-locked house, and drove on. Eudora came in with me while I typed off several copies of that prayer which starts, *"Lord, make me an instrument of Your peace."* I would tack one over my desk, I told her, and another over the kitchen sink.

Jane would keep one in her purse and one on her desk at the office.

We would keep a copy by our bed, and earnestly pray it the first thing in the morning, the last thing at night.

Even as I typed the words, "Grant that I may not so much seek. . .to be understood as to understand; to be loved as to love," it came to me that the whole prayer was a simple plea. *Think less of yourself and more of those around you.* And with a flash of insight I knew why I was so tired and grumpy. Not from any burden of work, nor what I thought impositions, but from the weight of my own inner resentment. And it was that grudging disharmony which acted like brakes on a piece of machinery.

I resented interruptions during my writing time—but wasn't I really to blame for there it was up to me to order my days better. Even saints had to have a time for concentration. If I set myself a time and place for working, when I was through I could give ungrudgingly of myself to the family—even to vacationers wanting hot baths and cold drinks and sandwiches and sunburn lotion.

Eudora was looking over my shoulder as I typed. "Where there is injury, pardon—" She broke out desperately, "I can't forgive him. I can't even forgive myself for being such a sap. When I think of how I offered to keep on working to make a home for his

81

kids—how I swallowed his excuses for years—and then to be tossed off like an old shoe—" her voice broke, "Everyone at the office knows. I feel bruised at the end of a day. I hate him so much I lie awake at nights, almost praying that every misfortune in the book will come to him—and her—"

"Oh, gosh, Eudora," I murmured. "That'll poison you."

"It has already," she admitted raggedly. "I cry over nothing. I can't sleep—I can't pray. My stomach's upset. I eat aspirin for my headaches. It even makes me mad, somehow, to hear other people laughing. I'm bitter as gall."

CHAPTER 21

A Two-Thirds Happy Ending

August 1954

Tonight our month was up. I was so excited, as if I were to finish the installment of a serial.

A month ago, three of us had pledged ourselves to follow that prayer of St. Francis of Assisi which begins, "Lord, make me an instrument of your peace,"—the prayer which, in essence, says, Forget yourself; think of others around you.

The three women were Jane, sixty, widowed and wealthy, but tight-lipped and tight-living and constantly complaining of loneliness and neglect; Eudora, a business woman in her middle thirties, bitter over being jilted; and I, grumpy and out-of-sorts because life bullied and drove me, until I had little left for the writing which is my livelihood.

In a sort of deadlock of desperation we had grasped at that prayer as a way to make ourselves and our lives over.

My problem was the least of the three. Though my life was crowded and cluttered, it was rich. Only my own attitude, my organizing of my days needed changing. My life needed weeding out, whereas Jane's needed seeding with new interests.

But poor Eudora! To plan for years to marry a man, named Howard, who suddenly married another. To have everyone know of the jilting. That is the most bruising blow a woman's heart and her pride can suffer. Eudora needed immunizing against corroding bitterness.

During the month I had brief contacts with both Jane and Eudora, though we made no final reports on our spiritual gains or losses. A neighbor asked me if I knew of anyone living near the V. A. hospital who would rent a room to an out-of-town Mrs. Cobb, who was anxious to come in and visit her hospitalized son. I thought at once of Jane's big house with its three extra bedrooms, only two blocks from the hospital, and of Jane's plaint of lonely days. . .Yet when I telephoned Jane and asked her, she said she wouldn't think of renting rooms and having strangers tramping through her house. . .

When I telephoned Eudora, she answered in a tired, strained voice. I explained to her about the worried, out-of-town mother and asked her if she knew of anyone with a room. Perhaps the pause meant that Eudora was thinking, "Grant that I may not so much seek to be consoled as to console." She said, "I'm not near the hospital, but their bus goes right by my apartment. I could drive her out in the evenings. She could use my bedroom. I've been sleeping on the living room couch and watching TV until late—trying to take my mind off my poisonous self. Yes, have her come here."

And now I was waiting for Eudora to pick me up to go to the book review. After it we three women would report our success—or failure.

Eudora still looked wan and tired, but her smile was less forced. She burst out as I got into her car, "It's helped—that prayer. And it's helped having that nice Mrs. Cobb with me. Bless her—always having a good meal for me in the evenings. Each night I take her to the hospital. Those poor fellows out there! I've been playing cribbage with one of the paraplegics. And I'm gathering up records for one of the wards. How about your baking a pie for me to take out?"

"I'm better at cream puffs. . .Is it still so tough at the office with everyone knowing about—Howard?" I asked.

"Not so bad now. At first I walled myself off behind hurt pride, trying to pretend I didn't care. But now, if anyone mentions it, I say right out, 'Yes, it was a blow when Howard threw me over.'" She laughed ruefully, "I still have a long way to go yet—I still have times when I hate him and his wife, and then I say over and over, 'Where there is injury, let me grant pardon.' But I do believe I'm over the biggest hump . . Now tell me about you."

"I took my undisciplined self in hand," I reported. "I moved my desk into a far corner upstairs where I can write mornings free from the telephone and minor interruptions. And I count on working from nine to midnight when things are quiet. Then, when I must stop to be a mother and grandmother and homemaker and hostess and neighbor, I can do it without feeling frustrated and griped. I'm happier—the family is happier. Oh, I've a long way to go, too—but I'm working at it."

We took Jane home after the book review. She didn't ask us how we had progressed, but started in querulously. "That prayer of St. Francis' might have worked back in the 1200s, but not now. For instance that part. 'It is only in giving that we receive—'"

"It's true," Eudora murmured. "I know."

"But I've only got so much to live on," Jane argued. "If I handed out to every Tom, Dick and Harry, who'd look after me?"

"It means giving of yourself, too," I suggested. "Like working at the St. Vincent de Paul bureau and giving parties for orphans."

"I don't have very good health," Jane complained. "If I wore myself out and got sick—why, I haven't a soul to take care of me."

So the selfless St. Francis was unable to change Jane. Perversely, she preferred her unhappy and lonely rut. . . There is a saying that a rut becomes a small grave. . .

No, neither Eudora nor I became saints in a month. But we did make ourselves over a little, and with ourselves, our lives. I like to think we have become better human beings, closer to those about us—maybe a little closer to God.

CHAPTER 22

It's Never the Same Again

August 1955

Our fourth son is due home now in about a week. Three years ago, looking so young, so like a Cub Scout in his uniform, he left for England and his stint in the Air Force. Every one of his letters these last months has been full of:

"I'm just counting the days till I get home.". . ."Is Betty still working up at the drugstore?". . ."I hope our old cherry tree is loaded with cherries.". . ."I can even taste your spaghetti and meatballs.". . .

I am counting the days, too. Already I have the Roman cheese and egg spaghetti in the house. Already the nearby members of the family are alerted for the gathering of the clan and the welcoming-home spaghetti dinner.

Yet underneath all my glad anticipation, I feel a certain uneasiness. I keep remembering the conversations of other soldiers who have come home, either on leave or after being discharged.

When our oldest son came home from overseas at the end of World War II, I remember him and one of his soldier friends talking over coffee in our kitchen.

"Going home is a dream," the soldier friend said.

"And that's all it is."

"That's right," our returned son agreed, "because all of us soldiers hold to the picture of life as it was when we left. We get home—then everything's changed. It's sort of a jolt to find it isn't the way we dreamed it would be."

Then our second son returned after three and a half years in a Japanese prison camp. I prayed that his homecoming would not be too disappointing, too jarring. In his absence his father had died; a brother and sister had married; he even had a tiny nephew named after him. Yet he had acquired—perhaps by his own grueling hardships—a grateful acceptance of life as it was.

At Christmas time he received a card which he read with a rueful head-shaking.

"It's from a fellow named Monahan, who was interned with me," he said. "You know, Mom, over there in prison, the fellows couldn't talk about anything except going home. Monahan was from a farm in Arkansas. He was always telling how his mother would see him coming down the road, and start whipping up pumpkin pies; how his brother would have their guns ready to go hunting. He would plan jokes he'd play on his young sister, and how he'd see all his old girls at the Saturday-night dances. I used to say to him, 'Look, you've been gone a long time. Don't expect to find everything the way it was when you left.' But he always said, 'Things don't change back there. It'll be just the same.'"

My son handed me the card which had just come from Monahan. It read: "Got home in time for Thanksgiving. My brother is married; he and his wife are running the farm. My mother and kid sister have moved to California."

I ached for poor Monahan and his vanished dreams. If only he had the wisdom to say to himself, "This is the way life is. It can't stand still. Even if I had come home and found everything the same, it still wouldn't be the same because I'm different. I left a boy. I came back a man."

You can remember, can't you, your first returning after you left home for school, or perhaps a job?

I can. I left the homestead and came up to the city to go to high school. A homesick country girl, I started looking forward to going home for Christmas when school first started.

And then, after the first excitement of being at home, I felt restless and let down. Our nostalgic memories have a way of dressing up things in such glamorous hues. I found that our prairie water had a mineral taste, and that the bed I shared with my sister wasn't as downy-soft as memory said it was. Even as Monahan, I had dreamed of our Saturday-night dances. I went, but I didn't fit in the way I had. Life had changed; I had changed. There was no moving back into the person I had been before I left.

I have seen so many soldier sons return that I can almost foresee this son's going through it. At first there'll be the glad exuberance of being home, and then he'll start to say, "Man, our old gang has sure broken up.". . ."Did you know that Betty is married and has a baby?" He'll try on the clothes he left and find he has outgrown them. He'll say, "Sure seems funny not to have Tommy around." (Tommy is the youngest who recently went into the Marines.) I'll have to explain that we took out the old cherry tree because one side of it was dead. "But this new one is beginning to bear," I'll add.

This is the time for parents to stand by. For mothers to realize that the mother-son relationship has subtly changed. Even though our son has been under orders, still he has been on his own. He is no little boy now to be bossed about. He has been weaned. Now we must have ready the more solid fare of understanding, of faith in whatever he wants to undertake.

There will be restless, let-down days for the returned

soldier while he relinquishes his looking backward for a new looking forward. We must help him to realize that all life is a series of "commencements," of open doors.

No, these boys can never come back and find it the same. Something has been forever lost. In every move we make, something in us dies; but so is there something born.

Sad? Not any sadder than any growing. Not any sadder than the cherry blossoms' falling to make way for the fruit, or one door's closing, when another waits to be opened.

CHAPTER 23

Hold it Up to the Light

June 1956

My mother had a word she used constantly—
"sleazy." Today most people pronounce it to rhyme
with "cheezy"; my folks rhymed it with "crazy."

I can see Mother yet at the dry goods store, picking
out material to make into dresses for herself and us
three girls. She would feel the material between fingers
and thumb, hold it up to the light. Some bolts she
would push aside, murmuring "Sleazy," meaning that
they would not stand up under suds, sun and hard wear.
"Now this will wear well," she would say—and buy it.

And I think, too, of my first "boughten" dress, which
I picked out myself when I was 15.

I didn't feel the material, or hold it up to the light. I
was too enamored of the nosegays of pink roses in it,
the pink ribbon sash, the lace yoke with the bertha-type
ruffle. This was to be my best dress for church, box
supper, the Fourth of July picnic.

I paid dear for those pink roses. They, as well as the
green leaves, faded and ran over the white background
and the lace yoke, even though Mother had tried to
set the colors in salt water. It wasn't even a solid pink
dress but a nasty shade of henna, with faint tracings of

91

flowers and leaves. The ribbon sash turned too limp for stiffening with sugar water. The lace yoke was far holier than I. That was a bad summer for me and the dress I was stuck with.

It seems a pity that it took a decade or two, and the equivalent of many henna dresses, before I, like my mother, began to discriminate between the sleazy and wearing well. The bright and perky curtains I have put up, only to have the iron go through their ruffles after the first washing. The shiny patent leather slippers I have worn out of the store, only to have them crack and fall apart before the summer was over. Once I bought a hat with a very fetching aigrette sticking up on the front of it. I wore it in a high wind, and came home to find only a wispy question mark on the front of the hat where the aigrette had been. All the little glued-on feathers had literally gone with the wind.

Mother used the term "sleazy" for people, too. "They're a sleazy outfit," she would say of one family on the plains who draped their washing on barbed-wire fences instead of putting up a clothesline, who let their raft of hungry dogs forage on the neighbors' chickens. To say that people "wore well" was highest praise. I remember when one of the prettiest, most sought-after girls in the country married a quiet, plodding man, and my sister said, "Imagine Teresa marrying *him*," and my mother defending him, "Jim will wear well."

And Jim has.

How many times in life it behooves us to finger a fabric and hold it up to the light. Books, put out by book clubs with glowing blurbs—"complete serenity"— "mirroring life." But held up to the light, the stories show up as only apologies for backstairs assignations or sex aberrations. All their skillful writing, their quoting of great philosophers are still only the pink roses and the lace yoke. Plays built around a man's tippling, his cheating on his wife, both of which always seem good for a laugh, but certainly sleazy fabric to build a life on. . .The pretty promiseful religions that guarantee success and happiness in return for right thinking. . . How often we have seen those pink roses fade and run in the scalding wash of tragedy.

And people. A younger me was always attracted to the ones with showy qualities: the outstandingly chic, the life of the party, the successful—even the bizarre. But friends need to wear well, too. Not many of the well-dressed, the witty, the talented aren't solid and real underneath—just as many dresses with pink roses can be found which wear well. But it's not the showiness we lean on when our world is shaky under our feet.

It came to me as rather a surprise to hear that old word, sleazy, used the other day. A rather astute friend of mine remarked about another woman, "Polly is so sleazy."

"Oh, I don't know," I murmured. "It's just those foolish pretentions of hers. Always bragging about her family, always wanting folks to think she's more successful than she really is."

"That's what I mean. It's like the sizing in bargain taffeta. It's cheap—it's dishonest."

It's a good word to apply to ourselves now and then. Sleazy. How do our ideals come through when the fabric of them is rubbed between the fingers of day by day living, when they are held up to the strong light of making decisions. A little flimsy, maybe. Ambitions? We have to watch out for the garish and the false. The young man who says, "All I want in life is to make a lot of money," is reaching for one that won't wear either well or long.

And what are the qualities that wear well in ourselves and in others? Rather old-fashioned ones—integrity, loyalty, kindness. Perhaps the greatest of these is kindness. Kindness is sympathy, understanding, unselfishness.

Yes, I think one of the finest things that can be said of a person is, "He wears well."

CHAPTER 24

—A Friend, Indeed

February 1957

Pity for a friend comes easier than rejoicing. I used to think it was an Irish habit of rushing in with soup and sympathy and scrubbing floors for the unfortunate, and then,—if perhaps the unfortunate became rich or famous—of standing aloof and belittling him. But as the years have passed, I realize it is merely a human trait.

"A friend in need is a friend indeed." We like to feel that we are the friend in need. That we are the friend, indeed.

But when is a friend in need? Not always when he is sick or needy.

I know a writer on the West coast. For years she struggled with little or no success. Then she wrote a best seller that was sold to the movies for a hundred thousand dollars. . .Yet when I visited with her this past summer, she said, "That was the loneliest time of my life. All my real friends stayed in the background, leaving me besieged by strangers who wanted to sell me something, or do something for them."

"I imagined your being feted until you were sick of it."

"I was—in Hollywood, and by social climbers. But not by my own crowd. I'd hear of their impromptu get-togethers—but they seemed to feel I didn't belong.

One evening I phoned a couple of old friends. They were having folks in for a spaghetti supper—I could hear all the festivity in the background—but they didn't ask me to join them."

"Maybe they were awed by all that sudden money of yours," I tried to defend them. "Maybe they'd have been embarrassed to have you there when they were scrambling around to find enough plates."

"So I had a small fortune?" she answered wryly. "I couldn't go out and buy a party. So I sat at home alone."

And yet, I thought, those same friends would have rallied around her if her book had been turned down by publishers. They would have been loud in their sympathy. Maybe they'd even have had a spaghetti supper for her to cheer her up.

And then I thought back to a friendship I once had that dwindled and died, not because of the success of the friends but because of my attitude toward it. . . Years ago, when all our children were small, my husband and I went with a couple I will call the Smiths. How often the phone would ring about four of an afternoon and Mary Smith would say, "How about feeding the kids, and then you two coming over? I'm just sticking a chunk of ham in the oven." How often we'd call the Smiths on Sunday evening, "Come on over for supper and some bridge."

And then the Smiths began to shoot ahead of us in income and way of living. You know—a house in the Country Club district, a Persian rug that cost a thousand. Dinner in their home meant a candle lighted table and food in silver dishes passed by a well-trained maid. After-dinner liqueurs in fragile, imported glasses.

So that somehow I hesitated to pick up the phone and say, "Come on over for supper," when supper meant the pot roast left over from Sunday dinner, with children and dogs underfoot, and my leaping up and down to mop up spilled milk or bring in a battered coffee pot.

I told myself that our harum-scarum entertaining was no treat to them. But I was attributing to them my own uneasiness and smallness of spirit. I wasn't honest.

The truth was that it deflated my ego to be with them when they had so much more than we. The cruel truth is that it takes more magnanimity of soul to rejoice with a friend than to sympathize with him. For sympathy and pity and "doing for" the down-and-outer builds up our own ego. We are bending down from our superior heights. We even feel very Christian.

Our ego, our pride doesn't fare so well when a friend outreaches us. We even say, "Oh, well, now that he's on top of the heap, I'm not pushing myself on him."

Some years ago, an old neighbor of ours was chosen for the signal honor of "Man of the Year." The Chamber of Commerce chose him because of his diligence in putting through a housing program. With a little feeling of intrusion, my husband and I attended the banquet where the plaque was presented him with laudatory speeches.

Yet, when the ceremonies were over, the Man of the Year pushed through the crowded hall to shake hands with us and say gratefully, "You'll never know how much it meant to me to see old friends like you here. Gosh, all this fanfare—why, it knocks the pins out from under you more than getting fired from a job."

Big headedness may go with success. I know of only one person who became cocky and arrogant in prosperity. He, too, happened to be a writer whose detective stories sold to a radio network. Or perhaps it wasn't wholly prosperity, for a one time friend said, "It's not success that's gone to his head—it's whisky. This is the first time he ever had enough money to buy it by the case."

No, some people are not changed by a merited honor, or by public acclaim, or by great chunks of money. But the attitude of others often changes toward them, much to their amazement.

So, let's not be so afraid of being fair-weather friends that we are only stormy-weather ones. Let's be as generous in saying, "Oh, I'm so glad for you," as we are in, "Oh, dear, I'm so sorry for you."

CHAPTER 25

Your Money's Worth

April 1957

Last month my column was full of cautions: "Don't buy too much. Wait for the luxuries. Be sure you get your money's worth." I know it will seem quite inconsistent for me to urge now: "Go ahead and spend. Don't wait too long. Don't worry unduly about getting your money's worth."

But last month my enjoinings were for young people starting their married life. This month they are for the people my age who are already hampered by their own cautiousness.

We are the middle-aged. In truth, we are even past the middle milestone in life. And many of us are too fearful of spending money for the extras that would bring us happiness, comfort, or just plain joy in everyday living. We are too afraid of not getting our money's worth.

We moved to this present house of ours twelve years ago. It hasn't a fireplace. It is the only home we've lived in that hasn't had one. So for twelve years, I have missed and longed for a fireplace. Now I can get a fireplace unit installed. It is less expensive than a masonry job, but still it isn't cheap. . .Should I—or shouldn't I?. . .I think of folks gathered around the glowing coals on a blizzardy night, of someone saying, "Let's pop popcorn." And then some well-meaning friend will say, "You're paying a lot for something you could do without. Would you be getting your money's worth?"

What is our money's worth?

I think of Amy Sutton, who for twenty years has worked in a kitchen that is strictly 1919. One narrow window makes it gloomy. The sink is in the corner, with the drainboard on the wrong side, so that she must backtrack to put dishes away. Wasted cupboard space is given to a flour bin that holds two hundred pounds of flour. And Amy buys flour in five-pound sacks.

For twenty years Amy has been cutting out magazine pictures of modern and delightful kitchens and showing me how hers could be re-modeled. But her husband is adamant. "No sir. I'm not putting any thousand dollars into an old house like ours. If we sold the house, we'd never get our money back."

But wouldn't Amy have got it back a hundredfold in pleasure, and ease, in her lift of spirit every time she stepped into her bright new kitchen instead of her old drab one?

So many of my contemporaries live in old houses. It's true that the remodeled bath, the enclosed back porch, the window cut down to make a door into the yard, may not materially enhance the value of our property. But haven't we got our money's worth when we run water into a gleaming all-in-one tub instead of that coffin-shaped one, sitting up on its claw legs; in soaking up sun on a glassed-in back porch; in making backyard suppers possible by turning a window into a door?

And not only are we reluctant to spend money to make our houses more livable, but we demur and defer when it comes to a trip, a vacation, the visit we plan to our folks.

Three years ago, middle-aged Eleanor had a chance to go to Europe with an artist friend who "knew the ropes." For a whole winter Eleanor vacillated between, "I've always dreamed of going to Europe," and, "I'd be spending money without anything to show for it."

But she went.

Not long ago I asked her, "Have you ever regretted

taking your trip?" Her face lighted up. "Oh, no. That trip did something for me. I may have less in my old age, but I'll have it to look back on."

And clothes. How often do we of the tight purse-strings try on a coat or a dress or a hat which, to quote the old cliché, "does something" for us. Yet some inner guilt makes us turn away and buy another which is a few dollars cheaper. We are never wholly satisfied with the substitute. We would have come closer to getting our money's worth if we had bought the costlier one.

Oh, it's not easy for us who have clenched dimes tightly in our hardscrabble years to let loose of dollars now. . . Arnold Bennett, the English novelist, said at the peak of his success, "Poverty is still in my bones. I find myself walking when I could take a cab for a shilling."

(By the way, did you ever notice how everyone has his pet economy? I know a man who thinks nothing of feeding quarters into the slot machine at his club; but let one of his family leave a light burning, and you'd think it was blazing their way to the poorhouse. A woman writer, with three bestsellers to her credit, spends hours cutting up pages of old manuscripts and stapling them together, when scratch pads are three for a dime. Myself? I can't bear to buy more than one pair of stockings at a time. I'm the kind who thinks that runs don't show in sheer nylons—especially if I turn them on the inside of the leg.)

No, I am not saying that we should be so spendthrift that old age becomes a grimmer specter than it already is. I am only saying that there are different ways of getting our money's worth. And that vitamins for the heart and soul are often as necessary and more rewarding than those for the body.

Money is merely a medium of exchange. If we invest it only to bring in more money, we still haven't got our money's worth. It is only when it brings greater comfort and happiness for ourselves and the ones we love that we have "value received."

I believe I'll order that fireplace for our living room.

CHAPTER 26

Same Old Track

January 1958

I keep thinking of an old square-dance call, "Pass right back in the same old track—"

For so many years I envied people who lived a planned, ordered, uncluttered existence. I especially envied a friend I shall call Natalie Smith because Natalie's planned days were never blown to bits by the unexpected.

As long as I have known them, Natalie and her husband get up at six, and have breakfast on the dot at seven. He goes to work and, if Natalie has a club paper to write, she settles herself in the study with the phone muffled to prevent its shattering her train of thought. Her doorbell seldom rings because over it is posted, "No Peddlers or Solicitors, Please."

She is a most efficient housekeeper—meals planned a week ahead; never a dirty dish cluttering her sink. I used to bask in the peace and quiet when I had lunch or tea at Natalie's. One time when she visited me, the house was suddenly rocked by an explosion in the basement. It seems that our boys and some in the neighborhood had decided it would be cheaper to make their own fireworks instead of buying them for the Fourth.

I even envied Natalie all the little niceties of her daily living: flowers on the coffee table; the matched set of cups for tea, different ones for coffee. The guest towels in the bathroom that fitted into its lovely decor; the smooth and manicured back yard in which we sometimes ate lunch.

What a contrast it was when I returned to the Weber domicile.

With six children, and five of them boys, there was often a carp or a turtle in our bathtub. Our back yard was pocked with caves. Makeshift tents were built over the clothes lines. Dogs cluttered the yard with bones, and dug around the lilac bushes. (I wonder why stray dogs and waifs of cats always gravitate to us. And why all the cats turn out to be prolific mothers.) There was the usual dose of fan-tail pigeons, lizards, chameleons, and white mice that liked to hide in shoes.

We could never have meals on the dot with all the comings and goings. Nor could I plan menus a week ahead when we never knew how many extras we'd be setting the table for. Or who would be staying over-night—or had stayed.

. . .One Sunday morning when the youngest was about three and the older boys were in their teens, I had occasion to grab up the little fellow and rush him to the bathroom upstairs. The door I tried was locked, and I kicked on it and bellowed out, "Open, in the name of the law!" It was opened by a startled young man I had never seen before. He had come home with one of our boys after a late date the night before.

No, and with boys taking turns at dishwashing, the mortality rate of cups was so high that we were fortunate to have enough to go around, matched or no, with handles or no. But most of all I envied Natalie her tranquil, undisturbed hours. What progress I could make in writing if my time wasn't so snatch-as-snatch can.

But there were sieges of measles, pink-eye, and mumps. And birthday parties which were more important to a child than my reaching a story's climax. I nursed babies and scribbled out plots. I packed paper, pencils, and unfinished manuscripts in with baby nightgowns and diapers when I went to the hospital to have a baby. My "study" was sometimes the bedroom, a corner of the living room, or the kitchen where I could leap up to stir the Spanish rice. I didn't dare muffle the phone. I might miss a call saying that one of the children had been hit by a car. But "someday," I told myself, when the children are grown, and life isn't so hectic and jumbled, I will have long, unbroken hours to write. I'll write more—and better, be an efficient, orderly and immaculate housekeeper.

The time came. The top four children were married and settled in their homes. For about a year, while the two younger boys were finishing their military stints, I was a widow living alone.

Did I become a different person with flowers on the coffee table, and every dish clean and in place? Did I bask in the quiet and peace, and keep regular writing hours? I did not. I washed dishes only when I ran out of cups, I'd write on a story, or read, or work a double-crostic till two or three A.M. and then sleep until the phone or doorbell routed me out in the morning. I was seldom alone. "Stay with me," I'd urge friends or relatives. "I've got beds just crying to be used." Or I'd call up somebody and say, "I'm baking cinnamon rolls—Why don't you come over?"

And now?

The two younger boys are home again. I keep a young grandson for weeks at a time, because his mother works.

My youngest son brought home two tiny pups, barely weaned, as a present for Mother. (Mother already had an itchy-footed dog named O'Malley, who has to be bailed out of the dog pound at intervals.)

The other son brought home a small cat he thought I'd like (we already had one) and called it Gus. (We've changed it to Gussie Mae—but the kittens are cute.) The boys are taking classes at our downtown college, and the classes are at all hours. Let me plan dinner at six, and one of them is sure to bang in at four, calling out, "Got to go back at five. What's there to eat right now?"

Again the house is full of boys, with the coffee percolator forever burbling, with my typewriter and dictionary used for school assignments, and the kitchen stove and Pyrex measuring cup for their experiments. Last evening—while I was trying to make dumplings— an experiment called for boiling a dime in nitric acid to make silver nitrate—and fumes that were choking.

But now I have had that "someday" to call my own bluff. I can no longer alibi or wish wistfully for uncluttered days. We are what we are. I know now that I am not the orderly, routine type. I will always be two jumps behind on dirty dishes, dusting, and matched cups and planned menus. I know now that I can write just as much—and as well—in the midst of hullabaloo. Life seems to have called out, "Pass right back in the same old track—." I'm glad.

That's the way I am, and that's the way I like it.

CHAPTER 27

Back in the Driver's Seat

September 1958

I remember about two and a half decades ago when Father was pushed out of the driver's seat.

I think I even know what brought it about. It was a revolt against the "authoritarian" father, that tyrant with the razor strop, and the voice that bellowed, "You'll do it because I say so." He was fairly hissed off the American scene by child educators, juvenile court workers and psychologists.

Especially psychologists. For almost every ill the human mind is heir to, they blamed this black villain of a father. He ruled by fear instead of reasoning; he stunted personalities instead of letting them flower; above all, he made his children insecure by not lavishing love upon them.

We wives and mothers, too, perhaps over-inflated with our activities in the man's world of job-holding and voting, did our share of pushing Father out.

At any rate, the American father, who didn't relish the villain role, changed. Suddenly he was saying, "I don't want my children to be afraid of me." Suddenly he became a pal to his sons, and an all-the-year-round Santa Claus to his family. When a problem came up he said, "Ask your mother," because Mother had read all the books on child training.

And now after some twenty-five years of petticoat rule, what do we find? An alarming increase in juvenile delinquency; children in so-called good homes running amok, and parents who bemoan, "I don't know what to do with John—or Mary." Now we find that women won a hollow victory when they wrested the authority away from the men of the house.

Some time ago I read an article about the low rate of juvenile delinquency in Italy. It was attributed to the fact that the Italian father actually ruled his family. . . .We don't have to look so far away as Italy. A judge, speaking at a luncheon meeting last week, said that in his three years with our Juvenile Court, not one boy from a Jewish home has been brought before him. "The reason is simple," he added. "Papa is boss, and the children have been brought up to know respect and authority."

And how our child educators and psychiatrists are recanting today! Now they are stressing the need for "male identification." They are saying that boys must find in their fathers the prototype they can admire and emulate. And that the girl child, too, needs a masculine ideal against which to measure her relationship with other males and, eventually, her selection of a mate.

This time the experts are right. It is normal for a small boy to brag to his playmates, "My father is stronger than yours," or "My father knows more than yours."

It is normal for a girl to feel that the male sex is there for leaning on, for protection, for greater wisdom. So that when her mother, a female, says in essence, "I'm the boss," this reversal of roles leaves her lost and confused. . .so lost and confused that later on she can well make a bad marriage or none at all.

We did away with the bullying dictator father. Heaven knows, we don't want a Barrett-of-Wimpole back. But we desperately need the authority he stood for. In our haste to unseat him, we quite overlooked something: *Children not only need authority, they crave it. . .*This same Juvenile Court judge said, "It's always the same story of the boys and girls we handle—either no father, or one who is too spineless to guide or discipline. These poor kids!—it's as plain as if they wore a sign on their backs, 'We *want* authority.'"

We have overlooked, too, that sternness and love can go together. In fact, sternness has more protective love than laxity, and the insecurity of today's child stems not from lack of love, but from that very lack of protective discipline.

And we were so sure those decades back that a child's *fear* of his father was a dreadful thing. Was it? Couldn't we do with more of it today? Wouldn't good healthy fear, either of parents or the law, deter these gangs of teen-age hoods who are a menace to society?

In some families it will take a bit of reshuffling to put Father back in the driver's seat. . .A young father said the other day, "I know I slough a lot of discipline off on the kids' mother. But I commute back and forth to work. I leave home early in the morning, and get back in the evening too beat to have problems dumped in my lap.". . .And a young mother said, "John is on the road four days out of every week. I can't save up all the disciplining for him, can I?"

But it is not the actual presence of Father in the household that counts as much as the *attitude* toward him. In his absence, the mother's attitude should be that of the helpmate carrying out his wishes. Instead of saying, "Of course you can get the bicycle," she must learn to say, "Your father will have to decide that."

Yes, now we see our folly in pushing Dad out of the driver's seat. Now, instead of hissing, we are clapping and crying, "Come back, we need you!" And it's high time. . .I'm even in favor of handing him back the razor strop.

CHAPTER 28

When is a Widow Well-Fixed?

February 1959

In the past decade a great number of my contemporaries have joined the ranks of widowhood. So that through the years I have heard again and again such remarks as: "Grace has been well-fixed—," meaning, of course, that Grace will have no financial worries. Or the regretful, "Poor Rosalie is left without a cent—," meaning that Rosalie will have to scrabble for a living.

But is a widow necessarily well-fixed if her purse is full?

Not always. No one could call Grace well-fixed although she lives on in her home in an exclusive district with a gardener tending her roses, and funds in the bank to draw on. For she has no inner fund to draw on, nothing she cares about enough to make her want to get up in the morning.

As a married woman, Grace's only interest in life was her husband, her one child, her home. She practically ran a taxi service, taking her husband to work, her girl to school, to riding lessons, to clubs. She thought her husband's thoughts, and carried the sample ballot he marked for her to the polls. She had been a musician when she was young but she never "found time" to keep it up.

The devoted wife and mother! It sounds laudable, but, alas, now that Grace is a widow with her daughter married, her props are gone. She fritters her days, complaining and tearful. If one suggests that she take up her music again, she laments, "My fingers are too old and stiff now." (If only she had kept them limbered up through the years!) Grace, one might say, had put all her eggs in one basket—and now the bottom has dropped out if it.

Rosalie, who was left without a cent, could not long afford the luxury of grief. She had to dry her eyes, drink an extra cup of coffee, straighten the seams of her stockings and look for a job. She reports at the Information desk at our State Hospital each morning at seven. . .There are many Rosalies who had either to find work or keep on with their teaching, selling of real estate, or taking dictation. One third of the 7,778,000 widows in the United States are in our labor forces. They are not as Henry James once cruelly penned, "Ragged relics, crumpled and useless."

I, too, am one of those nearly 8,000,000 women who, bereft of husband and the warm companionship of marriage, found herself in a kind of no man's land. Because of my husband's long illness, the children and I were not well-fixed. The very urgencies of daily living goaded me out of grief's lethargy. Meals to cook, Levis to wash, ear aches and ringworms to worry over. I had to gather my thoughts together and pound them out on the typewriter. Groceries, shoes, and the roof overhead depended upon it. Perhaps I would have wallowed longer in self-pity if life had not taken me by the scruff of the neck. For work and doing for others is the ideal therapy—especially for a woman.

The well-fixed Grace is still not a well-fixed widow because for too long she geared her life to doing for her daughter and husband and made no provision for the time when her hands would be idle and her heart empty. Unless she has the gumption to reach out for other ways to channel her innate desire for service, she will indeed become Henry James' crumpled and useless relic.

Now I am not saying that the widow who has to get out and hustle her own livelihood is more fortunate than the widow who hasn't a care about paying rent or taxes. I know other Graces, well-fixed with annuities, who are also well-fixed with mental and emotional outlets. They don't fritter and complain away their days.

One had dabbled at painting for years and, when her marriage was sundered by death, traveled to Europe and studied art. She came home and rigged up a studio and worked seriously at it. She helps young and needy artists to put on exhibitions—she even feeds the underfed ones. Another wealthy widow I know works at a day nursery for working mothers. She does more than put in specified hours there; she helps the mothers find better jobs and, one afternoon when I stopped at her home, I found her cutting up full-size blankets into smaller ones for cribs. . .Another widow, who always liked to cook, cans peaches and pears, makes preserves and pickles for an orphanage. And she keeps track of birthdays and always shows up with birthday cakes for the small motherless inmates there.

No, I am only saying that when widowhood comes, a well-fixed purse isn't enough to keep the last years from being lonely and dreary. It is rather a grisly fact to face that these left-alone years are in the cards for the average American woman because her life span is longer than her mate's.

The average age of a woman entering widowhood is slightly past fifty. But many are older and at sixtyish it is hard to get back into life's stream. If muscles are rusty, and fingers, like Grace's, are stiff, it can be too late. So it behooves us to be ready for the bereft time *before* it comes by keeping our minds stimulated, our hands busy and hearts open and outgoing.

The *Merry* Widow is a myth. I've never known one. I've known superficially gay ones, and vain and restless ones. But the ones who find serenity, in spite of that empty room in the heart that is never quite filled, are the busy ones, the *doing* ones, the ones who care enough about something to bounce out of bed each morning.

No, no widow is well-fixed, no matter how full her purse is, if her life is empty, and her days long.

CHAPTER 29

Cheap and Pretty

September 1959

The printed linoleum rug with its pattern of roses was so pretty and bright. Besides, it cost only a fraction as much as the same footage of *inlaid* linoleum. So I bought it for the kitchen of the first house we owned.

Yes, it was a cheerful and gay floor covering for a while. But all too soon the printed roses wore off from the frequent scrubbing and tramping feet, leaving spots of ugly black showing through. The edges scuffed and broke. I still remember the crack that ran from stove to cupboard, and became a cut which caught our feet, the broom and mop—and dirt.

A few years later when we ripped up the scabby thing, the only roses that still bloomed were on the untrod areas under the table and in the corners. This time we put down a durable inlaid linoleum which did cost many times what I paid for my ephemeral roses. And though it took a daily beating, it was still in good shape when, fourteen years later, we sold the house.

Unfortunately, I didn't learn this lasting lesson from my experience: That you get what you pay for and, all too often, the thing you get cheap comes dear. An old sage has said, "Good bargains are pick-pockets."

No, it took many years, many purchases later before I stopped reaching for the cheap and pretty. . .The dress for little Rosemary with a red, heart-shaped yoke. But on the first washing, the red of the yoke streaked into the white of the dress—truly a "bleeding heart.". . . The patent leather pumps for myself that were such a bargain. But one summer day on a long drive our Model T kept boiling until the floor boards were like a stove's top. I got out of the car to find that the "patent leather" tops of my slippers had melted right off the soles. . .

It seems a part of human nature, this desire to get a lot for a little, this unwillingness to pay a higher price for the real, the worth-while, the enduring. So we let limitations pick our pockets. Women, I believe, are more short-sighted than men when it comes to putting a price tag ahead of value.

Perhaps this same caring to get something without paying the full price explains why women—especially middle-aged ones—reach for all the pseudo-religious books that flood the market.

These books expound a bargain-rate, below-cost, bartering faith. You can have an abundant life merely by tuning in with divine harmony. You can draw on God's goodness to get yourself exuberant health, the perfect mate, and, of course, the upper-bracket job. . . . .Not a mention of the hours of drudgery, the training, the sleepless nights that success in any walk of life entails. . .no, you have only to saturate your being with confidence and trust.

Now no one can gainsay but that a happy outlook on life is better than a curdled one, which not only gets one no promotions, but often ulcers. But, according to these books, all life's blessings tumble into your lap by flipping a switch and bringing in God's goodness, love, generosity. Worries, misfortunes, griefs can never touch you if you sweep negative evil out of your thinking.

How adroitly the writers of these ideologies distort the words of Christ. How they delete and by-pass any of His sayings that have to do with pain and private Gethsemanes and bearing of crosses.

Often these seekers for the cheap and pretty and promiseful religion shop about for a church which gives it to them. Right now in our city there is a preacher whom I call Dr. Jones, though his real name is fancier than that, who is "packing them in." They tell me his services are theatrical performances with lighting effects, music—and always the spotlight on his handsome self.

I can think of five or six women on the fringe of my acquaintance whose faces light up when they tell of the "cute" things he says in his sermons. It's remindful of the way teen-agers went into squealing delight over Elvis Presley a while back.

It is his attraction, his entertaining personality that "packs them in." But is that faith? Where would the witty doctor's followers turn if he left for a richer parish in another city, or died of a heart attack?

I have known two women who absorbed and leaned on what we can only call a sweetness-and-light religion. One went through life up to the graying-hair stage, serenely confident that her days were rosy because she was in harmony with divine laws. Very fine while skies were clear, but when tragedy struck she had no foundation—nothing to hold on to. Now she is a confused, bitter and empty woman.

The other had worked out what she called her "Theosophy," which was a mishmash of the books she read and her own "inspired" thinking. Her life was full of real problems but she refused to admit or face them—something like a person sweeping dirt under the rug. . .After years of hoodwinking herself, she was bundled off to the mental ward of a hospital. You can't keep *on* sweeping dirt under a rug and pretending it isn't there.

And what does all this have to do with those of us whose faith is rooted in Mother Church? Just that we should be grateful that ours is not a cheap and pretty but sleazy religion. No preposterous promises of our going unscathed though this world. Just that we should be grateful that while it asks a price—sacrifice, prayer, attendance, keeping God's laws—we get in return a real and enduring Faith.

And one that wears well. One we can always turn to.

CHAPTER 30

Your Reading
Capacity

July 1960

You read current best-sellers but shy away from the classics because you feel they are over your head and are, at best, tedious and boring fare? If so, then I predict you are in for a happy surprise.

For years I passed them by as something only for scholars. I blame this one-time allergy of mine on the forced reading of certain ones when I was in high school. And what unpalatable chunks they were. *Tale of Two Cities, Ivanhoe,* Burke's *Conciliation with America* and *Silas Marner* which so soured me on George Eliot that it took me twenty years to tackle her *Adam Bede* and *Middlemarch,* It amazed me to find them a joy to read. (But *Silas Marner* remains on the shelf, gathering dust)

It wasn't until I had small children that I girded my mental loins and decided I must, if I was going to be a writer, read these musty books called the classics. I started with *Vanity Fair* because of the many references to its heroine, Becky Sharp. Resolutely, I set myself to it as though I were taking a cup of bitters.

I was carried away by it. I slighted the housework, and sat up late at night, anxious to see whether or not the little reprobate of a Becky got her comeuppance. (She didn't.)

It was such a joyful experience that I delved further. Samuel Butler's *The Way of All Flesh*. The children and I read *David Copperfield* aloud in the evenings, chuckling over Micawber and his "confidently expecting something to turn up." And shedding tears when Dora died.

Perhaps, because our present-day writers make a point of easy and alluring openings, we are often put off by the more leisurely and wordy first pages of the classics. My great love is the novel, *Kristin Lavransdatter*, by Sigrid Undset. Yet again and again when I press it upon someone, he or she hands it back with a sigh, "I just couldn't get into it." So now I urge, "Keep going, and you won't be able to lay it down. You'll live it. It's like a symphony with every human emotion being played."

And never was there a worse opening than in the masterpiece, *War and Peace*. The reader must flounder through a *soiree* in St. Petersburg with a dozen or so Russian characters, each one of whom the author calls by two or three different names. I've often wondered if many people didn't say to Tolstoy, "I got too lost in the first chapter of your book to read on." Because when his *Anna Karenina* came out four years later, this opening instantly caught the reader,

"Happy families are all alike; every unhappy family is unhappy in its own way."

"Everything was confusion in the Oblonsky house. The wife has discovered that the husband was carrying on an intrigue with a French girl—"

Classics have lived not only because they are worth reading, but because they are pleasurable reading.

Even though not the first to discover their delight, you feel as excited as though you were. I remember when I read Jane Austen, I felt like an early-day miner who has just found pay dirt, so that I wanted to shout out to passersby, "Just look what I found." I never expected

Pride and Prejudice to be so leaven with humor, or that the girls in it would be so like the girls of today. It was the same with Ibsen's *The Doll House* and Henry James's *Washington Square*.

It's fun going on a literary binge. I went on an Irish Renaissance once and read everything I could find by Yeats, Lady Gregory, John Millington Synge, the Colums—Padraic and Mary—another time it was Cardinal Fenelon. Not long ago I discovered Anthony Trollope. Settle down some evening with his *The Eustace Diamonds* which is a near thriller about just such a trollop as Becky Sharp. (No pun intended between Trollope and trollop.)

What about Shakespeare? Is he for the high-brows? We need not feel too humble about understanding him, for we are all unconscious Shakespearean scholars. Whenever you say, more sinned against than sinning, as sound as a bell, care killed a cat: each time you call something lousy, or say it was hard to laugh off, it is Shakespeare speaking through you. It helps in reading his plays to transplant yourself mentally back to the late 1500s in England, where as a "groundling" you would be standing or sitting on hard benches around an aproned stage with no setting, and very little time wasted on stage business. Shakespeare's audience wanted high tragedy and low comedy and that is what he gave them.

And poetry. Why are we so apt to think of poets as a race apart? They weren't—and aren't. Kipling was a soldier. Our own Robert Frost is a farmer. Byron died fighting for a cause he believed in. Maybe we can't understand all of the poetry we read but, by keeping our pores open, some of it sinks in. Poets are word economists. How much [A. E.] Housman says of drinking: "Look into the pewter pot / To see the world as the world's not" And Francis Thompson's, "Lo, all things fly thee, for thou fliest Me," is a one-line sermon.

You will have your loves and your hates. Proust leaves

me cold with his vague meanderings. I must confess I can't wade through Dante's *Divine Comedy*, yet I've read and reread St. Augustine's *Confessions*. Henry Fielding and his "And now, dear reader—" technique enrages me. Once I thought Greek plays would be either ponderous or soaring, but before I had read a page of Aristophanes' *Clouds*, I was chuckling heartily at his earthy—often bawdy—humor.

No, don't underrate your ability to read the classics. Don't ever think they aren't about and for people like you and me. So go ahead and laugh and cry and be stimulated by the Great Ones.

CHAPTER 31

So You Want to Be a Writer?

September 1960

Throughout the years, I have heard so often, "I would like to be a writer." I hear it from the modish clerk in the dress department downtown; from the pink-cheeked housewife who solicits for the Cancer Drive. An army colonel in California writes that now he is retired, and has time for his memoirs. A retired school principal shows me parts of the book she is writing about her pioneer grandparents.

Each spring, during Career Week at our high schools, I meet and talk to graduates who "want to write." These earnest young men and women ask, "What does it take to be a writer?"

Voltaire said, "If I had a son who wanted to write, I should wring his neck out of sheer paternal affection."

Unlike Voltaire, I don't want to wring necks—or hopes. But I do like to dispel any too rosy pictures the beginners, whether young, middle-ages, or retired, may have about this writing business.

What does it take to be a writer?

It could almost be put in the form of one of these Yes or No quizzes we find so frequently in magazine supplements today. The grade-yourself kind.

Is it easy for you to put words on paper? It isn't for everyone. Often, even the most fluent talker turns wooden with a pencil in his hand. *Do you find words stimulating, exciting and joyous?* The other day when I found that the word "Sycophant" means literally, "a shower of figs," I was as delighted as a botanist coming upon a rare blossom. *Are you an omnivorous reader? Does the written word hold such lure for you that you even read the labels on catsup bottles?*

The answers to the above should be Yes. For words are the pigments the writer uses to paint his canvases.

Are you easily discouraged? Are you sensitive to criticism and rebuffs?

Unless you can check No on these, don't choose writing for a career. Go into dress designing, or insurance.

For, as a beginning writer, you will get rejection slips by the wastebasket. I remember a Sunday morning when I dropped down on my knees in church and started to say the Our Father; instead, I found myself murmuring, "We thank you for the pleasure of reading your manuscript, and are very sorry we must return—"

So few people realize that there is a technique to writing just as there is to playing a clarinet, or building a house. Would the clarinet player expect the public to pay to hear his first squeaky toots? Would we hire a builder who has only started to learn his craft? The writer, too, must serve an apprenticeship. He learns to write by writing. He sends out a bulky manuscript with high hopes. He sees it come back with sick despair. But he tries another story, another article, another play—

Because of this apprenticeship, the neophyte writer should have another means of livelihood while he tries his wings. Bill Barrett, novelist, had an office job until he got a firm toehold in magazine writing. Robert Frost says, "I am a poet because I am a farmer." Sinclair Lewis always advised, "Do something with your hands—sell potatoes or wash cars—and let writing take over your mind.". . .The times I've scrubbed floors, rocked small Webers, and peeled potatoes, while stories yeasted inside me.

It is because of this apprenticeship that I am sobered and saddened by the retired colonels and school principals. They had to work up through the ranks to become colonels and principals, yet they seem blissfully confident that writing a book is only filling pages. . .But, bless them!—I haven't the heart to discourage them.

And now comes the most important part of the quiz. *Do you have something to say? Do you feel a missionary zeal to communicate to others the things you have learned, suffered, or been ecstatic over?*

I have been writing and hobnobbing with writers for thirty-five years. I have seen many drop by the wayside because they couldn't take rejection slips or scathing criticism. But the ones of us who keep on, in spite of the uphill-downhill road, the streak of fat, streak of lean existence, are the ones who yearn to clutch at every reader's elbow with, "Listen! Oh, please listen to what I have to say." (What we say isn't world-shaking. It is only a small facet of life's beauty or blemish, but we so passionately want to share it.)

It is illuminating to see that the writers who have lived through the ages are the ones whose something to say had to do with the soul's well-being. Cardinal Fenelon and Thomas à Kempis with their plea, "Let God work through you." Tolstoy and his insisting through every word of *War and Peace*, "No side ever wins a war. The victor loses as much as the loser." And Sigrid Undset who has her character, Kristin, say for her, "For every sin, we must atone."

To be a writer takes a love of words; and the resilience of a new tennis ball to bounce back after being slapped down. And perseverance, perspiration and postage. Plus a long faith in yourself and the little or big gift God gave you.

And the encouraging thing is: If you really want to write, no amount of discouragement will discourage you.

CHAPTER 32

Spoon–Fed

October 1960

I should like to go on the record as being anti guest speaker. I am even spleenish about it. All too often I have been a guest speaker; all too often I have been a listener—and I am anti, you might say, from both sides of the fence.

In rural communities and small towns, I am sure that clubs must, perforce, make and participate in their own programs. But in the large city where I live, every study and garden club, P.T.A., Altar and Rosary and Author's League can't consider getting together without an outside speaker.

This is right in line with the *spectator* sports we decry. Right in line with the spoon-fed entertainment of young people today. "In my time," parents lament, "we made our own fun. We played the piano and sang, or had taffy pulls."

Yet the same lamenters sit on folding chairs in a clubroom or around a banquet table while guest speakers spoon-feed them entertainment or opinions on world affairs.

Last spring I was asked to speak on writing at a club of young Catholic college graduates of both sexes. As the personable and astute young man drove me to the meeting, he told me of their successful seasons, and listed the men, each prominent in his field, who had addressed them.

"Do you have a speaker at every meeting?" I asked.

Oh, yes, he assured me.

"Why?"

He was too startled to answer.

"But the primary purpose of your getting together is to know each other better. You are all college graduates with interesting jobs. The girl who arranged for my talk puts on style shows. You are a court reporter. You all have a lot to contribute. Why not have panel discussions among yourselves? You don't always have to import a speaker from outside."

I am sure he thought I was a heretic.

I am anti book reviews, too. Alicia, a career-woman friend, was telling me about one of her numerous clubs at which they have monthly book reviews.

"What books have been reviewed?"

She floundered vaguely, "There was one we laughed so at—something about picking daisies. And then one—let's see, it was laid in Italy, and someone was investigating someone who was proposed as a saint—" That, I gathered, was *The Devil's Advocate*.

Now let me give a behind-the-scenes glimpse of the guest speaker. . .Comes the date when I have promised to give "Just a twenty minute talk" to a luncheon meeting of the A.A.U.W., P.E.O., or V.F.W. I had said Yes three months previously. (You've noticed, I suppose, that you make a date ahead, confident that by then you will be beautifully *un*rushed?)

But the day before the speech, a writing deadline is heavy on my neck. Yet, worried about the talk, I spend the day making notes. I sleep with my hair in roller curls, and get up with a headache.

No writing is accomplished the morning of the luncheon, what with my being keyed-up about the speech, and giving myself a manicure. As I dress, a run looms in my best and only nylons. A hurried dash to the corner drug for new, I am picked up at eleven-thirty. At the luncheon I meet a horde of people whose names I fumble, and nervously gulp down food that doesn't sit well. . .By the time I am home again the day is shot—and so am I.

But don't think my views of guest speakers are those of a put upon guest speaker. Don't think for a minute I am berating women's clubs. No. I know too well the hot school lunches, the veteran's Christmas parties, the scholarship funds they foster.

I will even recant enough to admit that it behooves the League of Women Voters to hear different candidates air their policies. That during Fire Prevention Week, Mother's Clubs are benefited by the fire captain warning them of hazards in the home. That a priest talking to an organization of married couples gives wisdom and inspiration. I am only saying there is too much sitting in the bleachers and not enough do-it-yourself with in clubs.

A fortnightly club I know limits its members to twenty-four, just so each woman can put on a program once a year. One member gave a paper on the first fifty years of struggling growth of our city. Another, an illustrated talk on penstick drawings. And still another on her Cornish miner ancestors and with the help of the refreshment committee, served pasties and saffron cake.

If all the members of Alicia's club had taken time to read a certain book and formed their own opinions, and one of them had MC'd a discussion on it, I am sure Alicia would not have looked so blank as to which books they had been spoon-fed.

"You don't need an outsider to talk about it," I prodded. "Appoint a leader and get a discussion going. Come out with the answers.". . .She told me later it was the liveliest meeting of the year.

"He who would bring home the wealth of the Indies must carry the wealth of the Indies with him." Or in simple terms: You get what you put in. You don't put in much when you sit back and hear, "It is my pleasure to introduce—" And you take out even less.

CHAPTER 33

Attention, Teen-agers!

April 1961

"Oh, Mother, you're old-fashioned. Don't you know times have changed since you were a girl?"

I said it to my mother, and I'm sure she said it to hers. My daughter said it to me, and now her young daughters are saying it to her.

The answer to all you teen-age Jeanies and Sherrys and Linda Lees is, "Yes, times change, but morals don't—and human nature doesn't. You girls will pay as dear for easy morals as girls did fifty or sixty years ago."

You want to be popular with the boys. Don't think I can't understand that. I remember, as though it were yesterday instead of decades ago, that when I was going to a dance on the plains I was shivering with dread for fear I'd be a wallflower. (In case you don't know, a wallflower was the girl who sat along the wall while her more favored sisters danced.)

And you resent your parent's surveillance, their rules about getting home at a certain time because you are afraid it will make you less popular with the gang. I understand that, too. How I chafed at fifteen and sixteen because I had to go to and come home from dances with my older sister and her beau.

I remember, too, that when my mother mentioned the chaperons of her day, I hurled out in disgust, "Chaperons! They went out with bustles."

But have you ever thought that maybe the old-time chaperon made it easier? She made the decisions, she protected, she saved the girl from bitter regrets. Today, your conscience must be your chaperone. It's the old story of greater freedom meaning greater responsibility.

Our morning paper carries a "lovelorn" column, and again and again that old question is asked, "Does a girl have to be amorous to be popular?" The column's answer is always, "She'll have only short-lived popularity."

And Nancy, a college freshman, puts it like this, "I guess every girl worries about being popular and is haunted by the specter of being left out. So I was certainly confused when I started at the U about whether I was just too Victorian—I mean, there were a few girls on the campus that were called Hot Lips—and golly, what a wild rush the fellows made for them. They had dates stacked up—early dates, late dates, later dates. . . .And then I noticed that those gals didn't get asked to the campus affairs—the games and formals and firesides—"

Nancy, you see, had found the answer on her own.

It was the same in my day. There were the "nice" girls and the "fast." Through the years they have been called *floozies* or *speed-balls* or *pushovers*. You'll notice it's always the girl who is labeled, not the boy. And I'll tell you why.

Because it has always been up to the girl to set the pace.

And now we come to the human nature that doesn't change. Don't think, Jeanie, Sherry and Linda Lee, that your boy friends in T-shirts and jeans are different front the young me who courted more formally in white flannels and straw hat. Now, as then, the boy has reluctant respect for the girl who is not a pushover.

There is a why to that, too. The male creature unconsciously sees the girl he dates as the mother of his children. So he may have himself a fling with the Hot Lips girl but he seldom asks her to have Thanksgiving dinner with his family. He seldom goes in hock to buy her a diamond.

In this same lovelorn column another recurring question is, "Will I lose the boy or the man I love if I don't give in to him?" The columnist's answer is, "He isn't worth keeping if you have to go to such measures."

And, as though in grim proof of that answer, other letters pour in—desperate "What Shall I Do?" letters that run like this, "I went with a boy and we were so much in love. . .now I am going to have a baby and he won't answer my phone calls or letters—" or, "He has left town." There have always been institutions for unwanted mothers.

There have always been what are crudely and cruelly termed "shotgun weddings." Occasionally they turn out happily. More often than not they are drab and bitter affairs that scar the lives of all concerned. Millions of words have been written about the psychological and economic handicaps of forced teenage marriages. All these millions of words are only reiterating that old cliché, "It's the woman who pays." And also, "The child pays, too."

If only you Jeanies and Sherrys and Linda Lees could realize that in the boy-girl relationship it has always been and still is a man's world. As I say, it is the girl who is labeled Hot Lips. It is not held against the boy. Somehow, the world makes excuses for him. His chances for a good marriage are not marred. Yours are.

So don't pay too dear for popularity. Let your conscience

act as chaperon. And don't think your parents and elders are heartless old fogies who are trying to rob you of fun. Oh, no, Jeanie, Sherry and Linda Lee, we are only trying to keep you from learning the hard way the unchanging laws in a changing world.

CHAPTER 34

Marry in Haste

September 1961

Every morning I read the paper while I'm having breakfast coffee. And every morning I run an eye over the names and ages of those who have been issued marriage licenses. It is the very *youngness* of them that always gives me a pause. Fifteen, sixteen, seventeen, eighteen. Here is one this morning: Nancy W—(16) and Joseph S—(16).

In our State a boy under twenty-one, or a girl under eighteen must have the consent of parents to obtain a license. Why, I muse, did Nancy's and Joseph's parents give their consent? Was it a case of pregnancy and wanting to give the child a name? Was it a case of Nancy and Joseph hurling out, "We're in love. And we're going to get married whether you like it or not"?

What has brought on this epidemic of teen-age marriages in the last decade?

The sociologist, of course, attributes it to post-war prosperity. The notes my youngest son took on a lecture by his sociology professor read: "The present tendency is toward a steady lowering of the age of marriage. Compare ages today with those in the early thirties which was a period of economic depression."

Yet I am sure it wasn't the state of the national budget so much as the fact that prosperous parents are more indulgent and less grim than hard-scrabbling ones. The small Nancys and Josephs have been given tricycles, formals and cars, but little responsibility. They have been given few lessons in self-denial, self-discipline.

Many people, and I am among them, blame these too-early marriages on the deplorable custom of twelve-, thirteen- and fourteen-year-olds going steady. By the time the boy and girl are sixteen or seventeen, their interests, their outlook has become so narrowed that they have to answer the biological urge by a "Let's get married."

I can't help wondering how the marriage of this unknown Nancy (16) and Joseph (16) will turn out. We know already how pitiably many have not turned out at all.

A judge friend of ours all but explodes when you mention teen-age marriages. "Can't someone hammer a little sense into these kids to save them from wreckage later on? I wish it were compulsory for every boy and girl to spend a day in court and see the bitter, disillusioned, confused young couples who come up for divorce."

Our morning paper also carries a column of letters from the troubled and desperate to "Dear Mrs. Merryweather" and her answers. A good percentage of the letters are from these bitter, disillusioned, confused young people the judge speaks of.

I quote verbatim from one this morning:

"I got married at fourteen. Now I am nineteen and have four babies. I'm miserable. My husband acts as though he hates us all. He calls us awful names."

"The springs of our couch are coming through. I have to take a rug off the floor to cover them so two of our youngsters can sleep comfortable on it. I've started a divorce but I'm scared to go through with it, for how can I start on my own with four kids? Oh, God, how I need help!"

And how her children need help!

Mrs. Merryweather's answer was for her to stay on

in her Tobacco Road home where she and the children would at least be sure of eating. And she added, "It's a pity you couldn't have thought of all this when you were fourteen."

Like all epidemics, this one of too-young marriages is contagious.

We Catholics cannot afford to feel immune from it. It's true that our teaching nuns (God bless them) have tried to stamp out "Going Steady" in their schools. It's true, too, that our church makes rash elopements impossible by the publishing of the banns, the consultations with all the parties concerned.

Still when early marriages are in the air, a Catholic girl can be wheedled by an amorous swain into being married by a Justice of the Peace, with the idea that her folks will *have* to come around. I know Catholic parents who have reluctantly consented to the marriage of a college-student son or daughter when the pleas of "Why should we wait? Nobody else waits till he's through school" grew too insistent. And I know Catholic parents—now grandparents—who keep themselves strapped financially, and are tied down by baby-sitting, hoping to keep the early marriage of a son or daughter from going to pot.

One keeps wondering if there is any way of stemming this epidemic. No pat and easy one, I'm afraid. The inculcating of sober thoughts on marriage has to come early. It's too late when Nancy or Joseph announce "We're going to get married whether you like it or not."

Perhaps we parents should work harder to counteract all the "Amour, Amour" of movies and fiction. If only we could teach our children that while love is necessary in marriage, it isn't enough. It must be coupled with responsibility, sacrifice and denial. If only, by precept and example, we could hammer home that marriage is a union of a man and woman with the know-how, the grit to face their own problems and not run whining to parents—or Mrs. Merryweather.

The old axioms, "Marry in haste, and repent at leisure," and "When poverty comes in at the door, love flies out the window," were written in the bitter ink of experience.

CHAPTER 35

And a Ph.T. for the Wife

October 1961

Our university out at the edge of town has a number of housing units for married students. The pleasant, compact apartments have bed-living room, kitchenette and bath. They rent for sixty-five dollars a month, whereas a comparable apartment in our city—not under university auspices—would rent for around ninety.

Does this mean that university heads are providing housing at a low rate to encourage student marriages?

No, it is rather that our campus, as well as others throughout the country, have *had* to meet the widespread and growing trend of young people mixing marriage and education. You remember that up until World War II, it was a rarity for the wedding license to precede the college diploma?

Because the man is the future breadwinner, and because nowadays he cannot go far in the business or professional world without higher education, it is usually he who goes to work. It has given rise to the campus wisecrack about the husband coming out with an AB [degree] and his wife with a Ph.T., which means Putting Husband Through.

I even know a blatant young medical student who

announced, "I'm looking for a wife to support me until I'm in Residency." (He found one, too—an attractive and capable lab technician.)

There is a diversity of opinion among educators concerning this trend. A professor of anthropology shakes his head. "Early domestic life serves as quicksand for our scholars. If young men with brains don't postpone the responsibility of a wife and family, this country is going to be in a bad way." And he ends testily, "Sometimes I think we're running a marriage bureau, not a university."

Yet a dean of women at a teachers' college says, "I consider our young working wives courageous pioneers. They are creating a new pattern in our changing mores."

Magazines and newspapers play up this "new pattern."

Our morning paper recently gave a half-page spread to the star hockey player on the university team—a handsome, blond Viking—and his working wife. The published interview was with her. She was proud and happy to be helping her husband get his degree. And she was quoted, "Of course, we'll have to wait three years to start our family."

Right there is the flaw in the new pattern.

Because the student husband and working wife of our faith cannot say blandly, "We'll have to wait three years to start a family," and include drugstore contraceptives in their budget. . .this thwarting of nature, of nuptial vows, is not our Catholic concept of marriage. To put it bluntly, this practice is merely legalized adultery.

So that the new pattern makes undue hardscrabble for *our* young people. . .I think of Mary Ann, whose husband is taking the hotel, restaurant management course. H.R.M it is called. Mary Ann was able to work as cashier until a few weeks before her baby was born. Since then, she babysits for her landlady to pay for their made-over upstairs apartment. Her husband, even as all

H.R.M. students, gets work at banquets, smorgasbords and wedding receptions. "It's a tight squeeze," Mary Ann says, looking tired and bedraggled, "but we've only two more years to go."

For others the squeeze becomes too tight.

There's Katie, who made a radiant, flowerlike bride when she married Joe, with his horn-rimmed glasses, and his ambition for a law degree. Katie worked before her first baby came, and afterward, by parking him with another mother. Joe worked at a creamery part time. When another baby arrived, the two still scrambled to fit in jobs, classes and baby-tending. Joe's late-at-night work affected his grades. When the third child was on the way, and Katie's low blood count called for more rest, there was no alternative but for Joe to drop out of school and find a full-time job. He says, "As soon as we get caught up, I'll start taking night classes."

One can't help wondering if they will ever catch up. Or wondering why they couldn't have waited a year or so.

Yes, certainly these marriages where the wife puts the husband through college is a new pattern. Heretofore, the husband has been the provider, the head of the house. I hope I'm not the type of person to decry a custom merely because it wasn't done in what we oldsters call "my day."

I find nothing wrong in a wife working to help a husband. Wives have always done that, either in the home or out of it, but the one thing that stands out as wrong is that, in these student marriages, a pregnancy is a thing to be dreaded. Because a baby's coming upsets the whole applecart.

And all too often when the applecart is upset, the parents of either husband or wife—or both—are called upon to right it. They must turn into free baby-sitters, or draw on their savings. This seems wrong, too, to work a hardship on grandma and grandpa, who have reached an age when they would like, and have every right, to draw an easy breath.

We of our faith have our own marriage pattern: the setting up of a home and having children to fill it. And the new pattern the dean of women speaks of, where the student husband comes out with an AB and the working wife with a Ph.T. is second-rate compared to it.

CHAPTER 36

Is It So Smart?

July 1962

A woman friend of mine frequently baby-sits for the small children of a young couple in suburbia. "They're so hard up," she has often lamented, "that I feel guilty taking my pay." Yet she tells of one late afternoon when the husband phoned to say that a friend was bringing him home from work, and added, "Mack will expect a drink of Scotch when he comes in with me."

There was no Scotch and no money to buy it. His young wife reminded him that they were waiting for payday to have their washer repaired and to buy vitamins for the baby. "We've just got to get a bottle somehow," he worried. "I'd never hear the last of it from Mack if we didn't give him a drink.". . .It ended with the wife's driving to a nearby liquor store and wheedling the manager into taking a post-dated check, and returning with the Scotch.

A relative of mine works as secretary at a swanky dude ranch which I occasionally visit. During the busy summer, this ranch employs college boys and girls. Their idea of a good time is not dressing up and going to a dance or movie, but driving into the village for an evening of drinking. And the next day, sitting at the staff table, they delightedly discuss it. "Boy, was I stoned last night!" One of the girls is liable to interrupt with, "You were stoned? I don't remember a thing after someone dragged me away from the slot machine."

Nor is this attitude confined to the younger set. Not long ago at the supermarket a woman in her fifties was telling me that a couple we both know had celebrated their silver anniversary. "Don't ask me anything about it, because I went completely blotto before they even served dinner," and she laughed merrily.

Here we have a young couple who would work a hardship on themselves and their children rather than lose prestige by not offering a fellow worker the expected drink. We have a college contingent who think of having fun in terms of becoming stoned. (I am sure that if one of the boys or girls wasn't a drinker, he or she would follow along rather than be thought a square— or whatever the latest slang is for being different.) And a middle-aged woman who sees nothing shameful in getting blotto at a party.

Why? Because, for some reason, and ever since Prohibition days, it has been considered the smart thing to drink. It didn't used to be like that. In my early childhood in a small Ohio town, the saloon-keeper and his family were not accepted by what was known as the Best People; women averted their eyes as they passed the saloon lest they embarrass the man who might be seen pushing in or out of the fanning doors. My girlhood was spent on the Colorado plains where the nearest town had three saloons. Needless to say no girl or woman ever put foot in one. The men did.

But they didn't *brag* about it. The populace even looked with disgust on the sheepherder or occasional ranch hand who had to be dragged off to the livery stable to sleep off his load. We held dances over a saloon and, to be sure, some of the men made trips up and down the stairs. Yet no girl would dance with one who was under the influence of liquor. Getting drunk in those days was a disgrace.

This is not a lecture on the evils of drink. We all know them. Nor am I priggish about a drink for relaxation or conviviality. We all know, too, that the majority of people can either take it or leave it while others, once they start taking it, cannot leave it. These are the alcoholics society is worrying about. Statistics tell us that, for every alcoholic, the lives of five and a half other human beings are tragically affected.

So it is frightening to realize that drinking is becoming not only prevalent with the college crowd, but reaching down to our high-schoolers. Even though the law forbids serving or selling liquor to minors, there are still devious methods of procuring it.

And it seems to me that it is society's attitude—this attitude that it is the smart thing to drink—that is largely responsible.

For public opinion has a great deal to do with public morals. Divorces were far fewer when respectable society did not open its arms to the divorced man or woman. Perhaps being guided by "What will people say?" is not the highest form of morality, yet it does act as a check rein.

It is that old desire to be looked up to, instead of being looked down on.

Fifty years ago our young folks didn't drink because it put them outside the pale. Today it is just the opposite. Today our young folks are fearful of saying, "I don't drink," because—well, after all, when drinks are being passed, who wants to be a jerk?

What is both paradoxical and ironical about our "drinking is the smart thing to do" attitude is that it all but cheers along a person to become a drinker; yet once he's gone over the border from drinker to alcoholic, then society no longer thinks it is smart. Then we shake our heads in despair.

It's our whole indulgent attitude that needs changing. Perhaps a little old-fashioned disgust for excessive drinking is called for; and no apology for not serving liquor. And like all other problems, the heaviest burden falls on the parents in the home. A burden of precept, example and reasoning. So that the young person has been fortified by his own standards long before he reaches the age when someone says to him, "How about a little snort to liven things up?"

CHAPTER 37

What is a Good Book?

November 1962

Over the years I have asked myself again and again, "What is a good book?" I read rave reviews of books on the best-seller lists, and listen to friends, "You must read such-and-such. It's simply wonderful." I read the book and say, "Yes, it's well-written and interesting but that's all you can say about it."

And perhaps someone will challenge, "What do you call a good book?"

Over a hundred years ago a writer, Herman Melville, gave us part of the answer:

"To produce a mighty book, you must choose a mighty theme. No great and enduring volume can ever be written on the flea, though there are many who have tried it."

And many who are still trying it today.

Our contemporary novelist, William Faulkner, died earlier this year. In this short and powerful speech in accepting the Nobel Award in Stockholm twelve years ago, he also gave part of the answer:

"The poet's, the writer's duty is to. . .help man endure by lifting his heart, by reminding him of the courage and honor and hope and pride and compassion and pity and sacrifice which have been the glory of his past."

"The poet's voice" (and this means writer's also) "need not merely be the record of man; it can be one of the props, the pillars to help him endure and prevail."

I must confess it is hard to reconcile what Faulkner said a writer should write with what Faulkner himself wrote. I have recently reread some of his books. And it is there, the heroism, the sacrifice, and the honor, but his meaning is so lost in miscegenation, idiocy and brutality; in his long, tangled, incoherent sentences that the average reader, which I consider myself, can scarcely glimpse those props and pillars he speaks of. A writer's first duty, I feel, is to make his meaning lucid. A reader should not have to fumble in the dark and make vague guesses. I see no virtue in such books as Joyce's *Finnegans Wake* which need a "pony" for interpretation.

Many of our best-sellers today by writers like O'Hara, Cousins, Weidman, to mention a few, are about human fleas flitting here and there (especially from bed to bed) utterly devoid of conscience of free will, but with over-developed glands and undeveloped hearts and souls. To these writers the very word "moral" is practically a dirty word.

These are our so-called "realistic" writers. Let a book jacket carry the blurb, "Revealing Realism," and you know you're in for clinical details or rape or sodomy, or sordid minutiae of poverty and degradation. But if realism means, (Webster) "Fidelity to human nature and real life, as opposed to romanticism which inclines to the sentimental and extravagant," aren't they being *un*realistic to depict slime but never sunlight? We find realism in its true sense, which deals alike with courage and cowardice, love and lust, faith and despair, in the Bible and on up through Shakespeare, Tolstoy, Dickens, Hawthorne and Undset.

Then we have authors who turn out a *Peyton Place* or *Lolita* which is blatantly aimed at getting a fast buck from the gullible public. The sad part of it is that the writers of both these books have the gift of writing well. Yet both pandered to humanity's baser instinct for money and these writers, Faulkner says, are laboring under a curse and I say they are a far notch lower than the prostitute.

Don't misunderstand me. My idea of a good book is not one depicting only sweetness and light. Life isn't like that. Life is full of bitterness and blight. We humans are frail and vice-ridden creatures. But, unlike the flea, we have a heliotropic urge to grope and reach to the light, just as the sunflower turns to the sun.

So that a good book, no matter how sordid, should still give our tentacles something to grasp and fasten onto.

Dostoevsky is not a Pollyanna writer. Yet it is said of him that he had only one background in everything he wrote—the soul.

The reader unconsciously identifies himself with the characters in a novel. If he is to attain greater dimension, he should identify himself with someone greater or kinder or more spiritual than himself.

You read Harper Lee's *To Kill a Mockingbird* and you long to have the quiet courage of the lawyer who defended the Negro in spite of the prejudices of everyone else in the town. . .In *The Edge of Sadness* by Edwin O'Connor, you suffer with the priest who was defeated by his addiction to drink, and you rejoice in his victory and gain wisdom along with him. . .You are as unable to resist the stubborn faith of the German Nun in Barrett's *The Lilies of the Field* as Homer, the itinerant Negro. You put the book down, believing that faith will still move mountains—or build a chapel. . .As you read *The Devil's Advocate* by Morris West you are warmed and stirred by greater compassion for human frailties along with the Advocate and, even as he, you, the reader, come closer to God.

It is heartening that these books about man's goodness

have also been best-sellers; and heartening to realize that the last three were written by Catholics.

Even *Ship of Fools* by that master craftsman, Katherine Anne Porter, which deserves such praise as magnificent, allegorical, superb writing, still leaves one with a feeling of, "Oh dear, surely all human beings aren't so cruel, so prejudiced, so indifferent to evil, so callous to suffering as this shipload of people." She has written here "merely the record of man" and his shortcomings. If only she had given us something to reach for and hold to!

Reduced to its simplest terms, my definition of a good book is: One that helps us to be good by making us yearn to be better than we are.

CHAPTER 38

In the Midst of Life

March 1963

Editor's Note: This month's column comes from the heart of a grief-stricken mother. We hope our readers will ask God to comfort Mrs. Weber as she has consoled so many of us with her past columns.

The telephone wakened me that morning.

My daughter-in-law was calling from the next state to say that my son Bill had been hurt in an automobile accident. She spoke swiftly, jerkily, for she was hurrying to get to the hospital. She would call me later, she said.

I hung up, jolted, but still groggy. Though it was eight o'clock there, it was only seven here—and I am not an early riser. Shakily, I made myself coffee, trying to piece together all she had said. Bill had been on his way to work; he was paymaster for a road-building outfit. Something about a detour—and a foggy rain—and his hitting a low bridge abutment.

As I drank hot coffee, my confidence rose. Bill had pulled through a lot worse things than hitting a bridge abutment. Didn't we always say he lived a charmed life?. . .He was only a year old when we had our first scare. In the night, the plaster ceiling fell in on him and his three-year-old brother. The older one was screaming in terror when we rushed in, but Bill lay motionless in his crib, covered with plaster chunks. His father, white-faced, lifted his limp form and carried him out, with my mother moaning, "God have mercy—." But as we eased him down and felt for a pulse, the little fellow opened his eyes, yawned widely, grinned, and went back to sleep.

Again when he was twelve, and playing baseball on a corner lot, some of the players came running to tell me Bill had been hit by a bat. "We think he's dead," one of them sobbed.

He was still "out" when I got there. A man bystander was just saying, "I'll call an ambulance," when Bill sat up, looked around and said, "I'm next up to bat."

So Bill's car had slithered and hit a bridge! Probably broken ribs, and a stint in the Ft. Riley hospital, I told myself. It couldn't be as serious as another car accident when we never thought he'd pull through. . .

That phone call had come to us at midnight from Emergency at our city hospital; a voice informed us that he needed immediate surgery and because he was under age (17) we'd have to come and sign for it. I can see Bill yet, sitting on a table in the Emergency Ward with a nurse holding the deep gash on the back of his neck together with sutures and sidestepping the pool of blood on the floor. He was the color of gray paper, but again he grinned at his father and me, and said, "Now don't worry. It's just a cut from my head going through an unbreakable windshield."

Several hours later when the surgeon came out of the operating room, he shook his head grimly, "When I took the inner stitches, I could see the white of the spinal column. Another hair's breadth, and you'd have had a call from the morgue. . ."

Yes, Bill led a charmed life, I reminded myself.

Twenty-one years ago when the Japanese fired on Pearl Harbor, Bill (just twenty-one) was on Bataan with MacArthur. One look at the map showed how far—how very far—the Philippines were from the United

States, and how close—almost touching—they were to
Japan. That's when I started praying, "God keep Your
hand on his shoulder." Corregidor fell, then Bataan.
We heard the grisly details of the Death March on the
radio. For over a year we didn't know whether he was
alive or dead.

Because of Bill, I learned to really pray. I couldn't ask
God to protect my son without asking Him to protect
all mothers' sons. I couldn't pray, "Bring him back
safe," without forcing myself to add, "but give me the
strength to take whatever happens."

Three and a half years of starvation and abuse in a
Japanese prison on Taiwan. (It was Formosa when I
studied geography.) But he came back. His father
had died a few months before. Bill was yellow with
malaria. His normal weight was 175 pounds; he came
off Taiwan at 109.

A miracle. He was home safe. But he drove too fast; he
drank too much—and drink turned him into a fighting
Irishman. "God, keep Your hand on his shoulder."

He pulled himself together, married his wonderful
Marie (he called her Mert) and had a son. He took
intensive Japanese language training, and went back
to Japan as an army interpreter, with his wife and baby
following. But when the Korean War broke out and men
were needed who could handle a troop, he was ordered
there. More guerilla warfare, more hand-to-hand
combat. More telegrams from the War Department; he
was wounded in battle. Bill's letter reached me, "Don't
worry, Mom. They just dug shrapnel out of me." He was
back in the hospital for surgery. "Only a hernia from
lifting a jeep out of the mud," Bill wrote.

Another return. Another time of drinking, traffic
violations, fights, promotions and demotions, bouts
with malaria. Loyal Marie weathered it all with him.
There were two Bills. The old sentimental, family-
loving one with his humorous grin and swaggering
walk; and the restless, tortured, bitter one. "God, keep

Your hand on his shoulder."

He seldom talked of his experiences. But one night when he was visiting here, I heard the crash of lamp and bedside table, and a heavy thump as he fell out of bed. I hurried in, bent over him. "Are you all right?"

"I guess I was still fighting the war," he mumbled. He added with haunted eyes, "I've killed a lot of men."

"But it was either your life or theirs, Bill."

"I know. . .But there's one thing you can never forget—and that's the look on a man's face when your bayonet rips out his guts."

That morning after Marie phoned, I kept drinking coffee, and trying to reach her. No answer. It was like an old pattern, this walking the floor, praying, waiting for a phone call. Why were the pins always knocked out from under Bill just when he was building a good life? His twenty years in the army were up over a year ago. He went to a university and began studying to get a degree in accounting.

But at mid-term he had to be rushed to the hospital with viral pneumonia and the malaria that constantly bobbed up. It was the X-rays showing spots on his lungs that turned our days and nights into a nightmare of worried anguish.

They were finally diagnosed as fungus growth (another memento from the South Pacific) which every doctors said could be absorbed as he built up strength. The army hospital dismissed him but advised against his going back to school and that was a cruel blow.

He never built up strength, nor regained the thirty pounds he lost. . .

The phone rang at noon. It was Marie. "How bad is he hurt?" I asked.

A pause, and then the choked words, "He died."

Just two words. My ears heard them, but neither my mind, nor my heart could accept them.

I took the night train back. The many, many times I'd taken it before, always with a box of my peanut brittle which would crunch while we played cribbage. While his young son kibitzed. While Bill would say, "How about some coffee, Mert?" The whole night through the wheels of the train ground out, "He died. He died," but I still couldn't wholly believe it.

In the chilly dawn I got off the train at the little town near Ft. Riley. The many, many times I had climbed off that same train and seen Bill coming toward me with his swagger and welcoming grin. Only then did the full realization hit me that never again would he be waiting there to thump me on the back and pull me to him.

That was weeks ago. At first, I must confess, my faith was the feeble kind so that I could only think, "Maybe it was God's way." But the days, the long night have dragged on. And now when, with the habit of twenty-one years, I start to breathe, "God, keep Your hand. . ." it is as though He answers, "I did. I felt he'd had enough. I was there with him that rainy morning."

Through the tears and heartache and loss, it's solace to know that He doesn't make mistakes.

CHAPTER 39

Some Fan the Flame

June 1963

The obituary column in our newspapers recently carried the name, Blanche Young McNeal. She was 80 years old. All over the city, writers began phoning other writers to comment on it to add fondly, "She did so much for me. Goodness, I remember when I took her short story course and—"

Let me tell you about my "remembering when."

Just think, it was 38 years ago! I was in my mid-twenties with three small children, when my husband brought home the prospectus of the downtown university where he taught gym and intramural sports. Among the listed courses was one in creative writing . . .Have you ever thought of how seemingly small happenings can change the whole course of our life? . .

From the time I was ten I dreamed of being a writer. I had scribbled my way through high school. A few years previously, while recovering from a tonsillectomy, I wrote a story which sold to *The Youths' Companion.* (Are any of you readers old enough to remember that family weekly, long since extinct?) After that one sale I had said to myself joyfully, "Now I am a writer.' But alas, other stories I wrote were promptly bounced back. Discouragement, babies and housework had laid low and crowded out my writing dream.

Creative writing! I enrolled in the course, though it

meant finagling and putting off payments to scrape together the money for it. In those days the word baby-sitter was not part of our vocabulary, but a neighbor girl looked after the children on Saturday afternoons. There was always so much to do before I left, so that I have a blurred memory of myself racing the three blocks between our house and the car line.

But I can never forget coming back. On a streetcar that swayed and rocked over the long viaduct. I would be high in the clouds. At home, I would finish the washing I had put to soak—no automatics in those days—my mind seething and sizzling with story ideas. Now nothing could crowd writing out of my days.

Why? Because Blanche Young McNeal, Mrs. Mac as we called her, was our short story teacher, and she made me think I was a second Kathleen Norris, Mary Roberts Rinehart and Willa Cather all rolled into one. Her encouragement was the impetus I needed. Even though I've always been a late riser, I got up at four in the morning and wrote, wrote, wrote before the day's hubbub started.

The course began in September, and the following March I sold a story to *The Savior's Call*. The title of it was "Saint Anne's Smile"—which was almost symbolic, for Saint Anne, the patron saint of mothers, kept her smile on me. I sold again to *The Youths' Companion*, two more to *The Savior's Call*.

And when about this time Rosemary, the youngest of our three, came down with scarlet fever, I'm sure it was Saint Anne who saved me from being rushed to the "pest house" by getting the quarantine sign off just two days before the stork arrived with David. During the quarantine when I couldn't go to class, Mrs. Mac would phone me. I can still hear her say, "That idea sounds exactly like what the magazines are looking for. And no one can put the feeling and color in it as well as you."

So, alone in the house with Rosemary and her

light case of scarlet fever, I wrote story after story. I fumigated the manuscripts in a big lard can by burning a formaldehyde candle; and slipped out at night and mailed them. As far as I know, no editorial staff came down with a red rash.

I have thought often about Mrs. Mac. I know other teachers of creative writing in other universities. In all honesty, I must admit that many of them have a more scholarly background than she; they are more familiar with Greek dramatists, more glib at quoting the masters, and perhaps better critics. But they lack that rare and priceless quality that Mrs. Mac had of bringing out the best in a pupil. She was a living embodiment of Goethe's aphorism:

"If we take people as they are, we make them worse. If we treat them as if they were what they ought to be, we help them become what they are capable of becoming."

Don't think for a minute that everyone who took Mrs. Mac's course became a writer. Many were not "capable of becoming." The writing road is long, lonely, beset and dark. And so financially precarious that many have to forsake it for the regular paycheck. But for the ones of us who had a certain talent, she fanned the flames. She saw us not as the bumbling amateurs we were but what we might become.

Marian Castle was in the writing class with me. For years she wrote western romances for pulp magazines. It was Mrs. Mac who urged her to try the serious novel, which she did successfully. Mrs. Mac saw Florence Means as a writer of teen-age books for girls, and now she has something like 35 titles to her credit. Wilma LaSasso would never have thought of compiling her wonderful Italian recipes except for Mrs. Mac. Vernon Kurtz's fiction has appeared in *Extension.* You also chuckle over his short bits in *The Saturday Evening Post* because Mrs. Mac saw him as a humorist. (Our own Ed Mack Miller was a mere broth of a boy when we old-timers were getting started.). . .No, none of us are geniuses; just folks who live to write as well as write to live.

And I can't help thinking how all of us—wives, mothers, teachers, executives—could well take a lesson from Mrs. Mac. Who of us couldn't give a better lift to all the human beings he comes in contact with if, instead of taking them as they are, he treated them as the people they are capable of being?

Long live the Mrs. Macs of the world.

CHAPTER 40

I Read a Book

October 1963

Someone has said that a reader calls a book good if he agrees with what the author has to say. No, that is not my definition. I'd call a book good if we are jolted and stimulated into thinking thoughts we hadn't thought before.

Such is the book I have just finished, *The Doctor and the Soul* by a German psychiatrist, Viktor Frankl. This is not a review of the book. I only want to pass on certain ideas I found thought-provoking, even though I disagreed with some of his philosophy.

But it was refreshing to read a psychiatrist who emphasized the "will to meaning" (life's meaning) rather than the "will to power"; and who stressed not the "pleasure principal" but "spiritual needs."

For this man, unlike so many "Nut Doctors," does not reduce religion to the collective unconscious or to archetypes. He believes in God. Let me quote this from him:

"I was once asked after a lecture whether I did not admit there are such things as religious archetypes. Was it not remarkable that all primitive people ultimately reached an identical concept of God—which would seem to point to a God-archetype? I asked my questioner whether there was such a thing as a Four-archetype. He did not understand, and so I said, 'Look here, all people discover independently that two and two make four. Perhaps we do not need an archetype for an explanation; perhaps two and two really do make four. And perhaps we do not need a divine archetype to explain human religion either. Perhaps God really does exist!"

That's a good answer to keep handy as rebuttal for the know-it-all, pseudo-psychologists who prate about mankind creating God because of his helpless craving for a guiding power.

This writer lays heavy stress on the meaning of life. While imprisoned at Auschwitz during the last war, his conviction deepened that the ones who had a reason for living were able to endure far beyond the capacity of those for whom life had no meaning.

He differentiates between purpose and meaning. "The activity of an anthill can be called purposeful, but not meaningful."

But the idea that impressed me the most, and the one that has been moiling about in my mind since I put the book down, was his telling that it was the confused and aimless people, for whom life had no meaning, who beat a path to the psychiatrist's office. I suppose you could call them doubting Thomases who can't accept the divine pattern because they can't see it or reason it out.

That's where faith comes in. Says the doctor, "A domestic animal does not understand the reason of the purpose for which man employs it. How then could man know the *final* purpose his life has, what 'overmeaning' the universe has?" And he quotes: "God sat at the organ of possibilities and improvised the world. Poor creatures that we are, we men can only hear the vox humana. If this is so beautiful, how glorious the Whole must be!"

Yes, beautiful in spite of life's buffetings.

Yet it is not the world's buffeting of human beings that turns them into neurotics and would-be suicides. It is their own attitude toward the world. The constant plaint of the would-be suicide, said Dr. Frankl, is, "Life has nothing to give me." And his answer to that is always, "What can you give life?" Or, "Stop thinking of what life owes you and think instead: What do I owe life?"

I thought of that a few Saturdays ago when I was lunching with two friends.

One of the women, Carla, had been a writer until she was widowed ten years ago. Because a writer of short stories cannot depend on a regular income, she turned to teaching to support her family. She is in a school with a large Negro and Mexican enrollment. She takes on their problems. She helps them through bouts with our juvenile court.

. . .One weekend she devoted to a young teen-age couple (one-time student of hers) who came to her dazed and grief-stricken, and said simply, "Our baby died—and we don't know what to do." Carla took over all the details. . .

One hot day last summer I looked out to see her with a heavy tank and its spray attachment de-weeding our lawn. "I did mine," she said, "and I decided to do yours before I put all this apparatus away."

Pauline, the third at the luncheon, is also a widow with her two children married and gone. She is a well-educated, well-traveled, "well-heeled" woman. Compared to Carla's—or mine—her life has been smooth indeed. Yet she was the one who said as we lingered over coffee, "Life has certainly gone stale on me, and I've gone stale on life. I can't find much reason for going on."

Carla said gravely, "Maybe you've gone stale because you're not giving out enough."

Pauline flared up resentfully. She had always more than paid her way, she said. She contributed generously to charities and to her church. (She is a parishioner of a fashionable Episcopal church, where her idea of the Best People go.) "Nothing seems to come my way these days," she ended bitterly.

I thought suddenly of our old German gym teacher in high school who, when he put us through deep breathing exercises, would thunder at us, "Giff out from your lungs. How can you take in air unless you first giff out?"

Well, that was what the psychiatrist was emphasizing in the book I read, and what Carla was trying, without much success, to tell Pauline. Come to think of it, a carpenter's son started saying it almost two-thousand years ago when He urged, "Give, and it shall be given to you."

CHAPTER 41

I'm Against It

January 1964

I have a feeling that in this column I am opening my mouth and putting my foot smack into it.

Several months ago I received a bulky envelope containing many mimeographed pages listing in detail a week-long program of lectures and discussions. This particular week, it seemed, was being set aside as "Senior Citizen" week, and all these lectures and discussions were centered on his health, employment and family problems; and on ways to fill his leisure time with hobbies and social clubs.

Aside from the fact that, as I've mentioned before, the term "senior citizen" strikes me as an all-time high— or low—in euphemism, this whole program rubbed me the wrong way.

For I do not believe in segregation of any age group any more than you or I believe in segregation because of color, race or creed. To segregate means: to separate or cut off from the others or from the general mass or main body; to set apart; to isolate; to seclude.

Do you remember back to the time when teen-agers were just children of thirteen or fourteen, or young men and women of fifteen to nineteen? And then suddenly—wasn't it shortly after World War II?—our social workers, educators, and psychologists began putting great stress on the problems of our poor, confused, misunderstood teen-agers. There was a great scurry of providing recreation for them; and great urging of the home and court to give them sympathy, more leniency, less discipline. Little mention was made of responsibility.

As a result, our teen-agers began feeling that they were indeed an isolated and secluded class who could live by a different set of rules. And juvenile delinquency flourished.

Now, I am not saying that spot-lighting the problems of senior citizens will result in a rush of senile delinquency.

But I am saying that this attitude of "Ah, the problems you face from an unsympathetic world!" is not healthy or helpful. After all, the years of being sixty, seventy, eighty, maybe ninety, are as much a part of life as the teen years of young people. But these mass meetings for senior citizens are only part of the new over-all pattern of segregation of the old—or should we say of the old segregating themselves? Look at how apartment houses, homes, colonies and villages for the retired have mushroomed all over the United States, especially in the no-winter areas like Florida, Arizona and southern California.

Perhaps the compulsory ousting of workers at age sixty-five by schools, banks, railroad offices and other business organizations, along with the pension plan, and social security, has contributed to the general exodus from the "main body" of the world and into senior citizen habitations.

I look to see exposé books written about them and their inmates, just as we had books about suburbia and what it did to the residents. . ."These small cities of ingrown people—" writers described it.

Suburbia, too, is a form of segregation. Block after block of young couples with small children, and all in the same comparative age and income bracket. No doubt they, cut off from the "main body" of life, do become ingrown. But they are young. They aren't permanent fixtures. There has been, and still is, a sort of "dump the fruit basket" when it comes to selling homes, and families moving to take up life in other places.

It's different with the older man and woman entering a senior citizen apartment house, home, colony or village. Not all of them, but a great many demand a sizeable payment to "buy in," and this payment usually exhausts the capital of the purchaser. So that the old person is stuck there like a fly that gets one leg on Tanglefoot fly paper.

And that, it seems to me, is the deadly, stultifying aspect—the seeing the same old people day in and day out, year in and year out. Truly, a "till death do us part" situation. And how can we keep the pores of our minds, hearts, and souls open without the give and take with people of different ages, different outlooks and ideals? Old people have much to give the young, and the young have much to give the old.

Don't think I am unfeeling about the many oldsters who are in dire need of having someone look after them. My heart goes out to the frail, white-haired woman who said to me last week, "I was so alone, and tired of eating alone and sitting through long evenings alone, and knowing that when my arthritis got worse, I had no one to look after me,"

Don't think I am not in sympathy with the ones who have a horror of being a burden on their families. On a recent trip to the super market, I talked to the father of a schoolteacher friend; he is seventy-six, and he said, "Well, I finally moved into that new apartment for the retired near here. It's taken a load off my girl. She worried about my being alone since my last heart attack, but she had her teaching job. It's nice to know I can press a button and get help." Our old and helpless need looking after just as much as our young and helpless.

But what doesn't seem right is that men and women, and married couples who are in their mid-sixties and still sound in body and mind, still capable of keeping on in life's stream, pack up and move to a retirement apartment or village. We have one on the edge of town. "For the Young in Heart," is its slogan, and their brochure pictures a golf course, swimming pool, game areas, club rooms and hobby shops.

Yet I can't understand why the "Young in Heart" want to take up an abode where no child under twelve can spend the night. Or why they want a management making the rules and calling the turns for them as though they were kindergarteners? And isn't all this frittering away of days at bridge clubs and in hobby shops like the busy work kindergarteners do?

My not being in accord with this, I realize, is even more deep-seated than the feeling that for the old to mix only with the old is unnatural and dehydrating. It's that no one has a right to shed responsibility as long as he is capable of bearing it. To be sure, these retired people have earned the money to live in idleness, but so have they been more fortunate and blessed than others less fortunate.

I don't think anyone need keep up his daily grind when he has reached retirement age, or that he shouldn't let down and do some of the things he has always wanted to do, but I don't think any able-bodied person should say, "I've earned a life of ease, and I'm going to take it, and to heck with giving a helping hand to anyone else."

And oh, the many spots where a helping hand is needed! There has been much lamenting in the past years about our young people shirking responsibility; much head-shaking over the new jobseeker and his choosing a position that gives security, rather than one that calls for initiative. Well, our senior citizenry is certainly setting an example.

It's too soon to know whether the years will be

satisfying or drab for all the residents who have flocked to either swanky or just comfortable retirement homes or villages. But, I repeat, I think all this segregation of older people cheats not only them but the rest of the world.

CHAPTER 42

Don't Kick
the Table Leg

February 1964

An old school friend of mine, Thelma, works with a marriage counseling bureau in another city. About two weeks ago when she was vacationing here, she stopped in to have lunch with me.

And because marriages and what makes them hold together or fall apart are vitally interesting, I asked, "Is there any one problem or cause that you'd say contributes to a marriage going on the rocks?"

"The problems are manifold—money, jealousy, over sexuality or frigidity, in-laws, disciplining the children. But the underlying use of their not being able to meet them is so often the same—immaturity."

"You mean that the couples are too young to be married?"

"Oh, no! Only a certain per cent are the very young. But so do we handle couples who have children in high school or college, which means that the parents are in their forties."

"What do you mean by immaturity, then?"

"The kind of immaturity that makes a child turn and kick the table leg when he whacks his shin on it. He isn't able to say to himself, 'That was my own fault,'

171

and watch out for it again. It's so much easier for us all to blame our hurt, our failures on something, or somebody else. Let's say it's the husband who comes to our bureau for help, and I interview him. He pours out his side of the story. To hear him, he is absolutely blameless, and it's his wife who is wrecking their marriage. I ask him to have his wife come in. She comes, tight-lipped, righteous, done-wrong-by, and she pictures a villainous or callous husband, with her the innocent victim."

"And then can you get them together and iron it out?"

Thelma shook her head. "It's not that simple. At first we work on them separately, to make him or her see that it isn't all one-sided. That's the biggest hurdle. It's as though the words, 'I am to blame,' stick in their throat. Occasionally, we get a man or woman who isn't capable of admitting it. And that's when it's hopeless. Because unless a human being can admit he's wrong, he will never be able to change." She laughed ruefully, "Sometimes I think it would be good to start drilling kindergarteners into saying, 'It was my fault.'"

As she said it, something rang a faint bell in my mind, but by then Thelma was launched into telling about her present case. . .

I make very good souse. It's made by cooking pigs' feet to the fall-off-the-bone stage and pickling them in their own jellied broth. And I always give some to an old family friend who is a retired judge.

When he stopped in last week for his rectangle of souse, I told him of Thelma's visit. I quoted her saying that the cause of many marriage breakups was because one or both parties was unable to say, "I'm to blame."

He chuckled. "She's right. I've often thought that we lawyers would starve to death if it weren't for that trait in human beings. Oh, I don't mean there aren't injustices, and innocent people lawyers have to defend—but let me tell you about the Metzer-Weld case. It was the first one that came to our firm when I started practicing.

I've never forgotten it.

"Forty years ago," he went on, "our town was bordered by small farms. And a farmer named Metzer had a Jersey cow that got out of the barn one night and helped herself to a little patch of sweet corn belonging to a neighbor named Weld. Weld locked the cow in his corral, and he and Metzer had a violent, name-calling scene the next morning when Metzer came after her. Weld refused to give up the cow till Metzer paid for his damaged corn, and Metzer said it was Weld's own fault for not having a tight fence. The battle was on.

"Now the road to town ran over a corner of Metzer's land, and on it was a dry sand creek with a bridge over it. The Metzers could get to town and back without crossing it, but the Welds couldn't, So Metzer and his half-grown sons went out with axes at dusk and hacked down the bridge. That night, Weld's school-teacher daughter and her date were coming home, and the car dropped into the creek bed and broke an axle. Well, that brought the boy and his family into the feud. The Metzer boys went to school to the Weld girl, and Metzer claimed she failed them out of spite—and I don't doubt that she did. For by this time there was bad blood not only between these two families but everyone else. The Metzer side—the Weld side. Plugged up irrigation ditches, burnt haystacks."

"How did they settle it?"

"It was never settled. It was one of the ugliest, longest drawn-out, expensive court hassles I've ever seen. It ruined both families, Metzer died before his time with a bad heart, and Weld took to drink. The community that had been a happy, friendly one ended with everyone at loggerheads."

"And all over a Jersey cow eating about twenty-five cents worth of sweet corn," I said.

"All over the fact that Metzer couldn't go to Weld that first morning and say, 'I was to blame for not fastening the barn door, but I will pay for the damage to your corn,' If he had, I'm sure Weld would have calmed down and admitted he was to blame, too, for not having a stronger fence."

He, too, shook his head. "I've cited that bitter mess when other clients come in all hot under the collar. Maybe I've lost a lot of fees by urging folks to admit they were wrong and make their peace." He paused, "And I've discovered this through the years: Because Catholics have been taught to say, *Mea culpa, mea culpa* about the time they're first-graders and make their First Communions, it doesn't come so hard for them to see it or say it."

Why, that was the bell that rang dimly when Thelma said children should be drilled into saying, "It was my fault."

The judge added gravely, "I've tried to get this idea across to people: If you can't admit to another human being or even to yourself that you're wrong, how are you going to admit it to God?"

CHAPTER 43

The Most Valuable Thing a Man Can Spend

March 1964

Yesterday morning Margie, who is in her early forties and has three school-age children and a salesman husband, stopped in to talk to me about her desire "to write."

When she was in college she wrote a two-act play which her sorority put on. "It went over big," she assured me, "and our drama teacher told me I had great talent for writing plays for school production, and that I should go on with it. But I got married and had a family, and I just never found time."

"You don't *find* time," I told Margie. "It's not something lying around to be picked up. You have to grab it by the throat before it slides away."

. . .Over thirty-five years ago when I had three small children and was expecting the fourth, I started to write. Because of my husband's off-and-on illnesses, my writing had to be not a hobby or avocation but a job. I didn't write what I felt like writing or when I felt like it. Necessity was my inspiration.

In order to have two unbroken-into hours, I set the

alarm and got up at five in the morning; being a born slugabed, this took every ounce of will power I had. During the day it was snatch-as-snatch-can to find time. I'd stop writing to nurse the baby, prop him up on the nearby couch with a typewriter eraser to chew on, and finish a paragraph. I'd put meatloaf and potatoes in the oven, and hurry back to the typewriter to finish the page. I worked late at night when the house was quiet.

I belonged to church, school and writers' organizations. Being the gregarious kind, my husband and I played bridge with one group, went to football games with another.

But I remember how when my first book was published, the outside demands increased a hundredfold. Would I give a talk to this club or that school? Writer friends brought me their stories to criticize. I was asked to serve on library committees. Invitations for luncheons, lectures, art exhibits poured in. Wouldn't I write the "funny dialogue" for a skit our PTA was putting on.

Thousands of years ago Theophrastus said, "Time is the most valuable thing a man can spend." Our own Ben Franklin put it more bluntly, "Time is money."

A writer's only stock in trade is time. I realized that I could not spread myself in all directions and still write. It is not easy for someone who loves people, parties, and being in the thick of things to weigh, sort and prune, prune. *No* is a hard word for me to say.

But I had to ask myself this swivel question: Will I get anything out of going there or doing this? Or will I be giving anyone else anything?

Certain affairs nourish the mind or heart or soul. I took classes in world literature, psychology, clay modeling. I kept up with old friends, helped on school reunions, and went swimming and on picnics with my husband and children. (Soon there were six.) We entertained because a houseful of company meant happiness for us all. Fortunately for me and my family, cooking has always come as natural to me as kicking to a cow.

Will my going or doing give anyone else anything?

I never slighted my mother's old friends who always thought of me as "One of Aggie's girls."

I never refused to talk to beginning writers, or criticize their manuscripts. (Alas, I have found that many neophyte writers want praise, not criticism.) I went to PTA meetings because my absence would disappoint the children. I couldn't give time to church bazaars but I tried to make up for it by giving books to their book fairs. When my husband was alive, we went to bridge and poker parties because he loved cards. I enjoy cribbage so much that I can always find time for that, though not for afternoons of bridge. Very, very seldom can I afford to let anything social break into a busy working day. (I loathe brunches.) I have always believed that no one should be so immersed in "making a living" that he hasn't time to live. And living means acknowledging birth announcements, going to weddings, funerals, First Communions, graduations, birthday parties. But there is so much "sucker growth" that needs pruning out else they sap energy and time— teas, fashion shows, a dawdling day of shopping, receptions, serving on committees when one is only dead timber. Each day has only so many unstretchable hours.

All this I tried to explain to Margie when she repeated, "I've always wanted to write plays. I'm sure I could if I only had the time."

For the past twenty years, as she admitted herself, her life has been a hectic round of cooking, home decorating, trips to the supermarket, chauffeuring the girls to music lessons, her boy to Junior League baseball and football, and all of them to the dentist, and to the doctor for shots. She tends the lawn when her husband is away, and is publicity chairman for one club, ways and means for another. She is still active in her sorority, and hasn't taken time to read a book in years.

I am not condemning this role of a modern suburban

wife and mother, but I am saying it will be doubly hard for her to funnel her time and energy and concentration on one particular goal. It will mean setting Spartan rules for herself.

Will she ever have a play accepted by a publisher? Will she ever even finish one?

I don't know. I was luckier than Margie on two counts. I was never happy unless I was writing, and I had necessity as a constant goad. There is no better inspiration.

CHAPTER 44

The Men, God Bless 'Em

June 1965

There is one column which appears again and again, though with slightly different slants, in magazines and newspaper supplements. And that is the one which quotes certain men—usually successful in their field—on what traits they like in women and what they do not. It is always sure to catch the avid interest of every young or old female reader.

Because—let's face it!—we women like men to like us. Even a small girl plays up to her father, or goes to great ends to win her brothers' approval. She puts on her best smile and best dress for an eligible male, and cooks the foods her husband is fondest of. In a business office she doesn't mind being imposed upon by a fellow male worker provided he gives her an appreciative pat on the back.

It seems almost paradoxical that a woman considers it a prime compliment to hear that she's "a man's woman"; yet no male wants to be tagged as "a woman's man." There's another paradox, too. It is that the married man has wholesome respect—maybe even envy—for the bachelor; whereas the married woman, even though her husband is no prize, feels a certain superiority to her unmarried sister.

I've often wondered why. Because the Miss in front of a name doesn't signify that there weren't chances to change it to Mrs. It often signifies that she felt more duty-bound to take on family responsibilities. *Or that she was more discriminating than her best friend who couldn't wait to get a wedding ring on her finger.*

But to get back to these constant columns on what men prefer in women, and what wards them off. Even though some men prefer the intellectual to the homebody type, or the mountain climber to the knitter of sweaters, they all, by and large, agree on certain points as to what they *don't* like.

Now I, like most married women, have tried my hand at matchmaking. The times, the times I've invited an unmarried girl or widow friend to dinner in hopes of promoting a romance between her and a bachelor or widower friend. One of my worst failures was when I tried to pair off a quiet-spoken engineer with a librarian I will call Frieda. I saw Frieda as a warm-hearted, loyal—and lonely—woman who had much to offer a man.

But alas, she was also loudly argumentative and opinionated. She let no remark at the dinner table go unchallenged. I remember that when the evening was over my husband made only one rueful comment, "Frieda! How to win arguments and lose men."

And when an older spinster friend heard that the engineer had never even asked Frieda for her phone number, she said bitterly, "What did you expect? A man always goes for some empty-headed little chit who bats her lashes and tells him he's wonderful."

That's all poppycock. To be sure there are certain men who have to feel superior to women. I know one husband who was so jealous of his wife's acclaim as a playwright that she had to give up writing. But the average man with confidence in himself doesn't need to be fed that "You're-so-wonderful" bit to build up his ego. But neither does he want a lifelong companion to leap down his throat with a contradiction every time he makes an innocent remark.

What are some of the other traits these articulate men who inspire columns don't like in women? Our average hard-working man is leery of the prima donna whose every word and gesture fairly shrieks a "Just-look-at-me" vanity. My Irish grandfather always said, "It takes a vain woman to pretend she isn't vain." We all have vanity but, like a slip, it shouldn't show.

No man likes a bossy female. Again, alas, this is a trait that sometimes doesn't show up until the wedding dress is hung in the closet. Certain characteristics in a woman soften with the years, but bossing and nagging seem only to grow and sharpen.

And let me mention one other type that hurts herself with men: the off-color raconteur in a mixed group. To be sure her spicy stories bring hearty guffaws from the men. But men, even though they don't admit it, still have a streak of Puritanism where the fairer sex is concerned. The girl or woman may win a man's attention by ribaldry—but not a man.

What does the boy on a date or the man with "Object Matrimony" *like* in a girl or woman? Their lists run pretty much the same: A sense of humor, the ability to be a good listener. Good grooming without being flashy, a happy outlook on life, a receptive mind. Many of them mention, "A faith in God" and the living by it.

Do you realize that these very traits that endear a woman to a man are the very same ones that endear her to other women, to neighbors and children, and to fellow workers?

Let us go back to the warm-hearted but contentious Frieda. Some years ago when her parents died and she was faced with making different living arrangements, she suggested to a woman friend that they share an apartment. Frieda's friend explained regretfully to me, "I'm fond of Frieda, and I know what a fine person she is—but heavens, I could never live with her constant arguing."

And so because we want men to like us, we women are apt to be our nicest, our most pleasing and attractive self around them. That's fine. The men, God bless 'em, are important in our lives. But the point I want to make is this: surely our lives would be richer and happier if we cultivated this nicest and most pleasing and attractive self not only for the men but for everyone else we live with and work with.

CHAPTER 45

All Men Are Created Equal

July 1965

Two nights ago I came home from a dinner party in such a disturbed state that I couldn't get to sleep. The dinner-party conversation had turned, as it often does nowadays, to Civil Rights and the Negro. Of the eight men and women there, only two of us were on the side of integration and equal rights. And we were shouted down by remarks like, "Look at the violence that's come from letting them (the Negroes) get out of hand." "Educating them is only a waste of money."

"I believe in keeping them in their place." (Their place being down scrubbing floors or up waiting tables.) I lay wide-awake, wishing I had been smart enough to make the right answers, and realizing that heart convictions aren't enough unless you have the right words to back them up.

You've all read, I'm sure, James Thurber's *Walter Mitty* stories, in his imagination Walter Mitty lived through hair-raising adventures where he always emerged as the courageous, astute, all-conquering hero. In real life he was a meek and hen-pecked little man.

Now I suppose we all have a Walter Mitty streak in us. Let me tell you of my favorite Mrs. Walter flight

of fancy. It goes back many, many years—as far back as the time when a Dr. I.Q. had a radio program where men or women in the audience were tapped, and asked a question, and rewarded by a few dollars if they could answer correctly. (Does anyone remember that, "I have a lady, Dr."?) One of his programs happened to fall on February 12, and a man was called on and told by Dr. I.Q. that for every word of Lincoln's Gettysburg Address he could recite, he would be paid a dollar.
As I remember, the man was able only to fumble out part of the opening sentence.

Perhaps because I recited the Address on a seventh-grade school program, I know it by heart, and with a little memory nudging and backing and filling, can still recite it. On nights when I can't sleep, I like to imagine that I am on a TV network where I am offered a dollar a word—

And what do you think? There I stand and amaze the huge audience by my brilliant, unflattering rendition of it from the "Fourscore and seven years ago—" down to the very last "—of the people, by the people, for the people—" The applause is always deafening as I bow modestly again and again, and walk off with my 260 or more dollars.

So on this night when I was sleepless not only because of the bigoted remarks still echoing in my ears, but because I hadn't been able to refute them, I took recourse in my ego-building dream.

Lying there tolling over those poignant and powerful words, they suddenly took on new meaning—and a meaning as applicable today as when our gangling, sad-eyed, war-harassed president spoke them on that November day in 1863 after the battle of Gettysburg where over 23,000 Union soldiers were killed or wounded.

It's all there in his opening sentence,
"Fourscore and seven years ago, our fathers brought forth on this continent a new nation, conceived

in liberty and dedicated to the proposition that all men are created equal."

He didn't say "conceived in liberty for the white race." He didn't say or mean that only white men are created equal.

Abraham Lincoln then went on to mention the dedicating of a portion of the field as a final resting place for those who gave their lives that the nation—so conceived and so dedicated—might live.

But these are the meaningful words that perhaps we should all relearn by heart,

"It is for us the living, rather, to be dedicated here to the unfinished work which they who fought here have thus far so nobly advanced."

These are the words which remind us that the work is still unfinished and has been for a hundred years. And that, alas, we haven't done so well with "the great task remaining before us."

"We here highly resolve that these dead shall not have died in vain—"

But the dead—the honored dead—he calls them *have* died in vain as long as people go on saying, "If I were a barber, no law could make me cut [an n-word's] hair." Or, "I'd take my little girl out of school before I'd let her hobnob with pickaninnies."

"—that this nation, under God, shall have a new birth of freedom—"

That new birth of freedom has not yet arrived, even though there are hopeful signs that it's a-borning. It is not fully born as long as Negroes can be refused food and lodging, as long as obstacles are meretriciously created to keep them from voting; nor as long as police can club Freedom Marchers, or shots end the lives of participants. This new birth of freedom must needs be under God Who lived the brotherhood of man and love thy neighbor.

I am only a layman with heart convictions but not too well-informed on all the movements. But now I have a new reason for wanting to be letter-perfect in quoting Lincoln's Gettysburg Address. Not because of those soothing imaginings of myself amazing a TV audience, or for the imaginary dollars I amass. But because I can use it as refutation against the very vocal segregationists. And with those earnest prayerful words, no one need let himself be talked down.

CHAPTER 46

Pity Poor Mom

October 1965

About twenty-five years ago, as I remember, Philip Wylie's indictment of "Momism" came out in print. "Momism" meant keeping spoon-fed sons tied to apron strings and preventing boys from becoming men. His treatise seemed to launch the barrage on Mom by psychiatrists, social workers, educators, and judges—with even the clergy adding their bit. The stay-at-home Mom was blamed for coddling her children; the working Mom for neglecting them.

To this day, no matter what events make front-page headlines in our daily papers, you can still find in the back pages something like "Permissive Mothers Blamed for Child Delinquency," or "Judge Tells Clubwomen to Stay Home with Their Children."

But the item which filled me with a hopeless, you-can't-win indignation was the one in last week's paper which explained why some students were "under-achievers" and some "achievers." These are terms used by a team composed of a university psychology professor and a high school counselor in their studies. And under-achiever is a pupil whose IQ test shows him to be brighter than average, but whose grades are little better than average. An achiever is one whose grades come out where his ability would indicate.

Their findings (to be reported in scholarly journals)

were that a possessive, strong and domineering mother tends to make her daughters achievers and her sons under-achievers.

Now I ask you! What is a poor woman to do? Is she a chameleon who can be a Simon Legree to her daughters and then do a quick shift to Mrs. Milquetoast for her sons?

Through these past years I have known conscientious mothers who avidly and earnestly read books by psychologists on enlightened ways to bring up children. But the more they read, the more confused, harassed and indecisive they become.

A mother could read the boxed article with its heading, "Permissive Mothers Blamed for Children Delinquency," and think, "Oh, dear, maybe I shouldn't have let Timmy keep that poor little pup he brought home." She reads the piece where the worthy judge excoriates clubwomen, and she wonders guiltily if she should resign from the Altar and Rosary Society. Next she comes upon this one about under-achievers and achievers, and she murmurs to herself, "Maybe I'm turning Mike into an under-achiever by not letting him go swimming in the gravel pit."

"What am I going to do?" one young mother wailed. "Our dentist tells me to stop Mary from sucking her thumb or she'll have a malformed mouth. But a book by a child psychiatrist says children develop frustrations if you break them from it."

Psychiatrists and educators not only differ and disagree with each other but with themselves as times go on. For instance, this psychiatric consultant who blames permissive mothers for delinquency and who ends with, "It is better to err on the side of strictness than on the side of permissiveness," is a far cry from all the earlier warnings about inhibitions, psychic injuries or traumas from stern discipline or scolding.

It was about that time when a young couple came to call on me with their three-year-old son. He headed straight for the low table where I had set the teapot and cups and saucers. Instinctively, I cried out "No! No!" Both parents turned reproachful eyes on me, and the father said, "We never say *No* to him. It destroys the ego." (The fallacy of such reasoning is that the boy will hear "No" constantly as he goes through life; from playmates and teachers; later on from his boss and, no doubt, a traffic cop.)

I am a little weary of these so-called experts who assume that poor Mom is a nitwit without common sense or conscience. We all know there are some poor parents. We are constantly shocked by hearing and reading of child neglect and child beatings. But the mill-run of parents whom you and I know love their children and want only to do right by them.

They want to do even better by them than their parents did for them. And they are more enlightened. Nowadays a child isn't shut in a dark closet, or told the police will cut off their ears if he ventures out of the yard. We may deplore the old-fashioned parent who wielded the hickory stick in the woodshed, but at least there was consistency. At least the parent felt he was right, and the child knew where he stood.

It's this befuddled shilly-shallying of parents which makes the child unsure. He is not so apt to be dismayed by a whack with a pancake turner when he had tried his mother's patience beyond endurance as he is by her doing nothing because she isn't sure how is the right way to handle a perverse child.

Children are tough-fibered, resilient little human beings. They don't expect parents to be haloed saints. But they do expect and have a right to expect consistency and justice in discipline, honesty of emotion, and above all the feeling of being loved and part of the family. This much-talked-of security is simply a feeling of *belonging*.

So I have come to the conclusion that poor Mom would do better to take counsel of her own conscience, her own common sense and her own maternal instincts, rather than from the horde of critics and experts who are so glib at telling her what to do and what not to do. She will make mistakes—we all do—but at least they will be her own.

And remember that any decision is better than indecision.

CHAPTER 47

Wanted Today: Catholic Pioneers

April 1966

When I was a child, we lived in a little Ohio town in an almost solidly Protestant community. Our own small church was always closed except on one Thursday of every month when a priest from a neighboring town rode over on his bicycle and said Mass.

We moved from there to a homestead on the western plains because of my father's health; there, the nearest town—or whistle stop—claimed a population of a hundred and twenty-five, as I remember. It had three saloons, but no church of any denomination. They came later.

So I learned American history in public schools: "In fourteen-hundred and ninety-two, Columbus sailed the ocean blue."

I remember the thrill it was when later I learned that Christopher Columbus and his sailors knelt on the deck in their desperate hours and prayed the same prayer I often prayed: "Hail, Holy Queen, Mother of mercy—" I like to think that they had reached, "Turn thou, most gracious advocate, thine eyes of mercy toward us—" when the cry of "Land! Land!" was sounded.

I'm sure most of you readers learned much earlier

than I that the list of great discoverers, the trailblazers of early America, read like a Catholic Hall of Fame, Amerigo Vespucci, whose name was given to the new world, Vasco de Balboa, discoverer of the Pacific. Ponce de Leon, seeking a fountain of youth, reached a verdant land on Easter Sunday—Pascua Florida in Spanish—and that's how our southern state got its name. Ferdinand Magellan, admiral of the first fleet to sail around the world, and the first to pass through the stormy passage now called the Straits of Magellan. Hernando Cortes conquered Mexico, and also discovered California. (It must have been a hot day, for the name he gave it means "Hot Oven.") Sir George Calvert, the first Lord Baltimore, founded a Catholic colony in Maryland.

The missionary priest, Jacques Marquette, S.J., was more of a searcher for souls than for new territory. One biographer said of him, "God put love in his heart and a torch in his hand to light the darkness." When he set out from Canada with Louis Joliet and five other men in two canoes to find the upper Mississippi, his prime motive was to take the word of God to more Indian tribes. Imagine traveling twenty-six hundred miles of turbulent river in canoes! "Had all the voyage," the humble but indomitable priest said, "caused but the salvation of a single soul, I should deem all my fatigue well repaid."

Add the Cabots, Champlain, de Soto, Cartier, La Salle and many others to the illustrious and almost endless list.

These men are our true pioneers. The ones who followed in covered wagons to settle the countries they discovered were brave and hardy men (and women), but the trail had already been blazed for them.

And who are our great pioneers and trailblazers today, when there are no physical wildernesses to conquer, but spiritual ones even more daunting? Pope John and his successor, Pope Paul. It is as if God touched the shoulder of Pope John, that gentle, humble, rugged man with his loving heart, and said. "There is darkness in the world. Here is the torch."

Pope John launched the Ecumenical Council. And Pope Paul, also gentle, humble, and rugged in his own way, carried on.

Not many of us laymen and laywomen were able to follow intelligently all the technical discussions relating to the passing of documents, but the very word, ecumenical, means "worldwide, liberal, tolerant," so that none of us can fail to grasp the Council's underlying principles of greater love, greater understanding; the brotherhood of man. Or reduced to its simplest terms, a greater emphasis on loving God and our neighbor as ourself.

We are proud that we can claim these present-day trailblazers as our own. But pride isn't enough. We too are obligated to get out of our rut. (An old sage has said that a rut is a small grave.)

We might even paraphrase that provocative sentence in John F. Kennedy's inaugural speech: "Ask not what your country can do for you; ask what you can do for your country," to "Ask not what the Council can do for you; ask what you can do to carry on the spirit of the Council."

This getting out of our rut, this ceasing to be a ghetto Catholic, which means a sloughing off of in-grained prejudices and old habits, is not always easy. There are things we should do, and things we shouldn't. We can't think or say, "I don't like to do business with Jews." Or, "We're going to sell our house because a Negro family has moved into our block." It is not in keeping with the spirit of the brotherhood of man.

Loving our neighbor as ourself isn't as easy as it sounds, either. For it means that no matter how distant he is, no matter what his color or religion, we should feel the same sharp anxiety over his hunger as over our own. And do something about him. It may mean we must learn more about the *whys* and *wheres* of poverty in order to help.

Yes, we can well be proud of our past and present heritage, but it should never be a smug or complacent pride. It should rather be the humble pride of the missionary Father Marquette, and of our two trailblazing popes.

CHAPTER 48

The Cynic and the Optimist

November 1966

A few mornings ago, I was dawdling in the kitchen over a cup of coffee, thinking of my next column and how I could go about expressing my Thanksgiving thoughts in a different way. I wondered then how a cynic would react in a conversation with an optimistic writer, and my mind rambled on something like this:

Cynic: "What are you writing?"

Optimist: "I'm just making notes for a column on Thanksgiving."

"For heaven's sake, don't write about the Pilgrims and all their terrible hardships, and their chasing down wild turkeys, and making pie out of pumpkins they raised after the back-breaking toil of clearing the land of rocks—and so they bowed their heads in heartfelt thanks. Not that old blah-blah!"

"No, I'm not writing about that first Thanksgiving, although I've often thought that today when we buy turkeys, frozen pumpkin pies, and maybe instant mashed potatoes at the supermarket, the idea of giving thanks never crosses our minds. No, I want to write about our feeling thankful today because. . ."

"Are you kidding? With the mess the world is in today, what can you possibly scratch up to be thankful for?"

"For this growing concept of what 'thy neighbor' really means. You can feel and see it—this reaching out to people of all faiths and color. Our gradual moving toward a real Brotherhood of Man. Last week I gave a talk on writing for teen-agers at the University. It did my heart good to see Filipinos, Cubans, and Negroes in the audience; and all mingling casually and happily with our Anglo students."

"And does it do your heart good to read about the race riots? What about the bloodshed at Watts in Los Angeles? How does that further this Brotherhood-of-Man bit?"

"Terrible and tragic as it was, it served to jolt us to a new awareness. It focused our attention on the misery, the dreary hopelessness of their ghetto experience. Until then, few of us realized how sordidly poor, uneducated, and exploited those Negroes were. It made us more understanding, and cognizant of what can happen in an oppressed segment of our population.

"Let me tell you something else that shows the change in the general climate. Twenty years ago, a Negro family moved into a house two blocks from here. Almost overnight, that whole block was peppered with For Sale signs. A month ago, a Negro family moved into a house in the block behind us. This time every homeowner stayed put. Except for one of two diehards, all the neighbors accepted them. Oh yes, there are signposts all along the way to point out that the world—meaning human beings—is reaching out to its fellow man and its natural sequence, reaching up to faith and love."

"Maybe you don't read the papers. What about the juvenile delinquent who murdered his playmate? What about the scandals in Washington?"

"What I'm talking about you don't find in the papers.

It has always been true—the press plays up evil rather than the good, brutality rather than humaneness. That one juvenile delinquent makes sensational headlines, but there's no mention of all the teen-agers who have worked like buckskin mules all summer on the Head Start program. I went with two girls on one of our hottest days while they collected remnants from wholesale garment houses for curtains, bedspreads, and clothing to use in adult sewing classes. I know girls and boys who gather up carloads of small children to take to pools for swimming classes, or to the foothills for wiener roasts. These young workers get so carried away that they're out of pocket themselves buying gas, or maybe popsicles for the children. . ."

"Before you get so carried away yourself, let's hear about a signpost of humanity reaching upward. You'll be telling me next that our politicians in Washington don't put their hands in the till."

"Unscrupulous politicians have always put their hands in the till. But there again, the conscientious ones never make headlines. A man from Washington was telling me about the chapel in the Capital building. The chapel would be quite crowded, he said, before an important meeting in the House or Senate. That, too, does my heart good—to think that our men at the helm believe in the power and efficacy of prayer."

"And other signposts about mankind reaching toward the stars?"

"Oh, yes, and a very heartening one, for it proves what I've always believed—that humanity gropes and turns toward the light as surely as the sunflower turns to the sun. For the past eight or ten years there has been a fallacious turning toward Existentialism. I've read a lot on it, and have listened to our so-called intelligentsia interpret and misinterpret it: life was nothingness, an absurdity without meaning. But now who do you think has supplanted Sartre? Teilhard de Chardin. A college professor remarked not long ago, 'It is utterly unbelievable that the jet set has turned from the dark nastiness of Existentialism to de Chardin's more solid fare of faith and hope.' Whereas the Existentialist wallowed in what he called 'anguish of being,' de Chardin sees pain and suffering as developing a closer relationship with God. He stresses thought and love. And it's this *love* that is yeasting, and slowly breaking down barriers and bringing us to maturity."

Perhaps Cynic had heard enough, for she got up to leave. Her final word was, "Sounds to me like you had to scratch awful hard to find something to be thankful for." And Optimist's was, "Well, at least it's there for the scratching."

CHAPTER 49

Was the Mystique a Mistake?

January 1967

Perhaps many of you saw the program on Educational TV in which David Susskind interviewed four nuns. They were not only devout and dedicated women, but also articulate, personable and brilliant. Each one had a Ph.D. in a particular branch of learning. In fact, they were about two jumps ahead of their interviewer at all times.

It would be impossible to cover the whole interview, but one point of interest was their discussion of the changes of nuns' habits. I, like many others, had heard of this with a certain regret. It seemed to me that by discarding the voluminous black or gray garments and white headdresses, they were destroying the *mystique*, the world's image of the nun.

But that, as they bought out, is exactly their aim. The *mystique* of the nun was a mistake, one of the four said. The oldest of the Sisters, who had a beautiful saint-like face, explained that her habit dated back to the mid-1800s, and was a replica of the costume women of the world wore at that time, except for its sober shade. The whole idea was for a member of their order to be able to move about in the background and *not* call attention to herself.

With the passing of the years and drastic fashion changes, this dark, cumbersome attire does just the opposite—it calls undue attention to wearer. In any gathering today, a nun stands out like a blackbird—or penguin—in a flock of pigeons.

Another of the nuns pointed out what the author of *The Secular City* stressed: that only in anonymity can there be complete freedom of thought and action; that when any person has to live up to the "image" the world has of him, he is hampered.

Teaching nuns head art, literature and drama departments in schools and colleges. They direct both classical and modern drama; they attend the theater. And one of the interviewed nuns mentioned the self-consciousness they were bound to feel when, because of their presence, those about them squirmed in embarrassment at some of the off-color quips on the stage. (And what modern play is without them?)

A new concept of the nun's role today (aside from the cloisters) is that is to do good in the world by mingling with its people and its problems. And that by being individuals and using the talents God gave them they can all the better fulfill their vows of poverty, chastity and obedience.

This very word "obedience" was gone into on the interview. Being women of strong personalities, convictions and purposes, did they not find it hard, David Susskind inquired, to be obedient to all the rules laid down for them?

The nun with the saint-like face was prompt in answering that, too. No, she said, because any "community," which is their word for nuns of one order living and working together, must have routine to prevent chaos. Their vows of obedience, she explained, went beyond daily regulations and were to God and their conscience.

It was these vows to God and conscience that

prompted nuns to take part in the Freedom March at Selma. The four nuns on TV were in complete accord in believing that each and every member of the sisterhood must follow her conscience. It was not only her right but her responsibility.

This, to me, was the most enlightening, heartening, and provocative message of the whole program. This applied to all of us. They were saying what Emerson said: "Go put your creed into your deed." For a true Christian it isn't enough to *be* good; he must also *do* good. How else can we follow in Christ's footsteps?

It is so easy for most of us to feel that going to Mass and Communion, keeping fast days, and giving to charity is all that is required of us. But Christ's short life on earth was spent in doing for those in need. He cured a blind man. But how much effort are we making to cure the blindness of prejudice and bigotry which is the biggest stumbling block in achieving civil rights for all?

Again and again the New Testament tells of Christ "exorcising devils." Our modern-day devils are the injustices to the poor and to minority races. In my part of the country we have the itinerant workers who come up from Mexico to work the beet fields. The crowded, unsanitary squalor of a family of 10 in one small room is unbelievable.

Last summer a group of compassionate people tried to better these living conditions, and met only apathy from the townspeople. It wasn't until the leader of the group took the mayor and his council down to the wretched huddle of houses and pointed out the flies swarming about the filth said, "These same flies light on your children," that the town fathers decided to do something about plumbing for the ignorant, helpless workers. Thus the devil of callous unconcern was exorcised.

We women in the world are apt to be content with the image life gives us. We are the busy, self-sacrificing wives and mothers, the busy, important career women, even the busy church workers. All fine. But are we doing enough to make the world a little better?

Surely, in these perilous times we could give more thought to what the soft-voiced nun calls our responsibility to God and our conscience.

CHAPTER 50

And Now, Good-Bye

June 1967

There always comes a time when the best of friends must part. More than 21 years ago, as I sat in the *Extension* office with Eileen O'Hayer and Monsignor Lux, this column was launched. Those two were not only my bosses but lifelong friends. Now they are both retired, and Timothy Murnane, also competent and dedicated, is getting out a magazine which enlightens and stimulates Catholics in what is more than ever a changing world for us. His magazine is one we can all point to with pride.

Twenty-one years ago! I had been recently widowed, and the youngest of our six children was eight years old. Now he is married with two children of his own, A lot of water has gone under a lot of bridges, a lot of words through my typewriter, a lot of joys and jolts have added gray hairs to me and, no doubt, to you subscribers of *Extension*. I wonder if there are any of you who read those first columns in the spring of 1946.

Extension readers, God bless you! You soon became like family to me. You wrote, telling me of your own experiences and problems. Sometimes you asked for advice which I gave to the best of my ability. Some letters praised what I wrote, others lambasted. That was good, too; a boot in the pants never hurt anybody. I answered every letter except an occasional "poison pen" one.

A very wise professor at the university once told our class that there were two jobs in life in which the job-holder constantly grew. One was teaching; the other, being a parent. And I believe you can say the same thing of writing. For certain types of it, a writer must do research, interview specialists in the field to learn all he can about his subject. For other types of writing, he must probe into the human heart and soul, and in the probing he not only learns something but becomes something more than he was.

I can assure you that writing this *Extension* page for you had made me grow, too. Before I could shape up a column, I had to first clarify my own opinions, philosophy and faith, and, in so doing, I believe I became more thoughtful, understanding and kind. And because you readers were like family to me, I could write about the White Elephant shower I gave for the bride-to-be of this youngest son; I could sound off about the people who blame their shortcomings, even ill manners and vile temper, on an unhappy childhood. Even when stark grief struck, I could tell you.

It was when one of my sons met sudden death. I wrote to Eileen O'Hayer, telling her I couldn't possibly do the forthcoming column. How could I think of one, when all my thoughts were tears? But as the days passed, I felt a longing to share the sorrow with you who had been so close and understanding. I got out of bed (I had what the doctor called low-grade pneumonia), sat at the typewriter in my robe, and told you of this son with the swaggering walk and twinkling eyes, of his three and a half years in a Japanese prison camp, and the dice that always seemed loaded against him.

What I was really saying to you was, "It hurts so—it hurts so," and just telling you about it eased the hurt. Unexpectedly, your letters poured in—over a hundred of them—and your ready sympathy comforted me more than I can say. Thank you again.

Twenty-one years! Try putting into words what life has taught you in that time. You'd be amazed at what a diligent and thorough educator old Professor Life is. Let me do some random summing up of lessons learned, and see if you have learned the same.

It is a waste of breath to pray for "things." God is no Santa Claus handing out dolls and red wagons. One can only ask for strength, wisdom and courage to meet whatever comes, be it good or ill. . .The older we get the dearer friends and family become. No doubt old friends, like old gold, are best, but we are never too old to make new friends. . .The hardest word in the English language for us old softies to learn to say is "No!" and make it sound like No, and not Maybe. . .

Even twenty-one years ago (when I was old enough to know better), I was unduly impressed by people with a sharp wit and a striking personality. Life taught me that the old-fashioned virtues which are not so showy— integrity, kindness, industry, gratitude and loyalty— wear better. A word about these last two. Is it because life moves so fast that we so easily let gratitude and loyalty go by the boards? "Gratitude is the music of the heart." Then loyalty must be letting others hear that music. . .

"No man is an island entire of itself," John Donne wrote some 400 years ago, which is another way of saying that our lives are beautifully, irrevocably, yet hopelessly entangled with other lives. I have learned the hard way that we, as individuals, cannot know, or even expect, happiness if someone we love is under a cloud. It is only when we can say to ourselves, "God never promised us a bed of roses. This constant heart-heaviness I must live with," that we gain not happiness, but a certain acceptance which is akin to serenity. . .

It is hard not to turn maudlin when it comes to saying good-bye to you whom I have known these many years, So I will say instead, "Hail and farewell, dear companions!" and "May God sleep on your pillow."

Acknowledgements:

Editing *One Woman's World* has been a decade-long journey, with many stops and starts along the way. I'm deeply grateful to Tom Weber (youngest son of Al and Lenora Mattingly Weber) as well as Tom's daughter, Nonie Weber Link, for their kind and generous support of this project.

Thanks to Thomas Gordon and Lisa Lagger of *Extension* for helping put Mrs. Weber's columns back into print. I owe a special thanks to Joy Canfield, founder of Image Cascade Publishing, who revived Mrs. Weber's fiction and championed this nonfiction work.

The intrepid Madeline Nathaus designed the book, and my dear friends Kari Sanderson, Sasha Schwenk and Aaron Vetch proofread it. Karina Corona undertook the task of transcribing.

Thanks to my friends and colleagues at Columbia College Chicago, especially Professor Emerita Norma Green, Professor Sharon Bloyd-Peshkin and Suzanne McBride, Dean of the School of Graduate Studies, for cheering me on.

Thanks to the Denver Public Library and its industrious librarians, who have helped me research Mrs. Weber's columns, photos and personal papers in its archives.

And lastly, this book would never have existed without the persistence, encouragement and ingenuity of my husband, Rob Elder. We've been through many book projects together, but this is the first one with my name on it.

About the editor:
Betsy Edgerton is an associate professor of Journalism in the Communication Department of Columbia College Chicago. She has an extensive career as an editor, specializing in business journalism; she's also an editor of nonfiction books. Her academic interests include the genre of "housewife writing" from mid-century magazines. She holds a bachelor's degree in journalism and English from Indiana University and a master's of arts in education from DePaul University. You can find her on Twitter at @BetsyEdgerton.

CPSIA information can be obtained
at www.ICGtesting.com
Printed in the USA
JSHW022308240721
17218JS00001B/26